Our Forefathers' Warnings

January 6, 2021, Foretold in 1796!

A Must-Read for All American Citizens and
Their Elected and Appointed Representatives

"The Baneful Effects of the Spirit of Party"
President George Washington 1796

B. Cylent Knowmohr

ISBN 979-8-89345-232-7 (paperback)
ISBN 979-8-89345-233-4 (digital)

Christian Faith Publishing
832 Park Avenue
Meadville, PA 16335
www.christianfaithpublishing.com

The quotes found herein are in the public domain based on the year of their publication and the dates of death of their authors.

Printed in the United States of America

Acknowledgment

I would like to thank my wife, Gayle, who endured countless hours of solitude while I was engrossed in researching, assembling, and rewriting this book at my desk *in the other room*.

Warnings from the Past Spoken by Our Forefathers

Contents

General Introduction

This book addresses the adversarial political conflict that currently infects our nation. It will present you with comments and warnings uttered by some of our more prominent Founding Fathers as to the dire threats to our nation that are inherent in divergent political parties, especially today when their respective leadership seems more concerned with party loyalty than the national good and foster irrational thoughts of states seceding from our union. Pay close attention to the warnings issued by our first president, George Washington, when he left office in 1796. His warnings, which he had hoped would have been repeated over the years, have been forgotten, contributing to the anger and distrust that plagues our government today.

The purpose of this book is to introduce you to a side of our Forefathers not often displayed in our history books—their fears for our nation under the arbitrary rule of opposing political parties. These eighteenth-century fears seem all too ready to manifest themselves today. The quotes of the Forefathers being provided are accompanied by their portraits, to allow you to see the face of the man who uttered the words you will be reading. This is intended to make the individual's statement more personal rather than just dusty words taken from history.

It is hoped that the opinions of the Forefathers as to one's obstinate adherence to a party might cause you, the reader, as a member of a political party—be it Republican, Democratic, Libertarian, Constitutional, Independent, Progressive, Conservative, or other—to take time to reflect *and think for yourself* rather than blindly following the rhetoric and propaganda of any respective political leadership. All too often, it seems such rhetoric and propaganda are directed at demonizing their political opponents, exalting themselves or their chosen candidates, and ensuring their own respective power and prestigious positions as elected members of "our" government.

I submit this book to all citizens but in particular to the silent majority of our nation who are fed up with the petty arguments that plague our political parties and delay needed legislation. Arguments staged for the sake of one party or the other coming out on top—a misplaced loyalty to a *party* rather than to the nation.

The current political climate and the upcoming 2024 election require that We the People demand that our elected leaders rein in their blind political allegiances and return to *their responsibility* to govern our nation properly. It is not *their* individual opinions, all too often biased by individual prejudices or *unmitigated party loyalty*, that ought to rule in governance. It is the consensus that we, the voters, both of the majority *and* minority, arrived at through compromise, which will achieve the goals we seek. The perpetual animosity and discord that inhibit our country from being properly and responsibly governed *must come to an end* before *we do* commit national suicide.

The Question Is…

To We the People…a question.

The history books that we use to teach our children depict our Forefathers as being larger-than-life individuals who, after defeating overwhelming odds, formed our nation, created our Constitution, and documented our rights in our Bill of Rights—some 233 years ago—and another who successfully defended those principles and saved our nation from division some seventy years later. They are viewed as monumental and historic leaders who lived long ago but have no relevancy today.

But what they *said* then still reverberates today. They were mortal men who themselves had fears for the future of the nation they had just founded. This included the mere existence of political parties, which they feared would lead to the eventual demise of our nation. One must surely admit, from today's bitter animosity between our two major parties, that they have split the relative tranquility of the nation and divided *our people, at least their radical and most vocal members*, into at least two separate and hostile camps. With the moderate majorities of both parties remaining mute, these irrational zealots from both parties have successfully inhibited the smooth and efficient enactment of legislation and have suppressed the required unbiased leadership, which all of our elected representatives are expected to provide.

I ask you now, as an American citizen who cherishes our Constitution and Bill of Rights and respects the right of every citizen to access those rights *equally*, to consider the following quotes and reflect on how vividly they apply to our current political turmoil some 233 years (1791–2024) later. Then ask yourself this question: are we, as a people, as Americans, clinging to an obstinate adherence to our political parties, leading our nation to its ultimate demise— just as our Founding Fathers warned?

Regarding Partisan Politics

Will They Be the Demise of Our Nation?
It Has *Already Divided* Our National Unity as a People!

[The Spirit of Party]
"The Great Idol"

"*The party lash and the fear of ridicule will over awe justice and liberty*, for it is a singular fact, but none the less a fact, and well known by the most common experience, that men *will do* things under the terror of the party lash that they would not on any account or for any consideration do otherwise...

Here is where the greatest danger lies—that while we profess to be a government of laws and reason, *law will* give way *to violence on demand* of this awful and crushing power...*the great idol*, it crushes everything that comes in its way."

Abraham Lincoln (1809–1865)
"Lincoln's Lost Speech," May 29, 1856
Bloomington, Illinois

(Sixty years after George Washington's Farewell Address in 1796.)

Where Did the Founding Fathers' Fears of Political Party's Corrupting Influence Originate?

Perhaps it was inspired by an Englishman six years prior to our own revolution in 1776, as the English Parliament, its equivalent to our Congress, was experiencing its own dysfunction. These were the times when the *Stamp Act* and other acts were imposed upon the American colonies of our Founding Fathers. On January 9, 1770, William Pitt the Elder addressed the English Parliament, stating,

> When then my Lords, are *all* the generous efforts of our ancestors, are *all* those glorious contentions, by which they meant to secure themselves, and transmit to *their* posterity, a known law, a certain rule of living reduced to this conclusion that instead of the arbitrary Power of a King, we must submit to the arbitrary power of the House of Commons? If this be true, what benefit do *we* derive from the exchange? Tyranny my Lords, is detestable in every shape, *but in* none *is* it so formidable as where it is assumed and exercised by a number of tyrants. But, my Lords this is not the fact, this is not the Constitution. We have a law of Parliament. We have a code in which every man may find it. We have the Magna Charta. We have the Statute Book and we have the Bill of Rights...
>
> It is *your* ancestors, my Lords, it is to the English Barons that we are indebted for the laws and Constitution we possess. Their virtues were rude and uncultivated, but they were great and sincere...I think that history has not done justice to their conduct when they obtained from their Sovereign *that* great acknowledgment of *National*

Rights contained in the Magna Charta; they did not confine it to themselves alone, but delivered it as a common blessing to the *whole people*…

A breach has been made in the Constitution—the battlements are dismantled—the citadel is open to the first invader—the walls totter—the place is no longed tenable.

What then remains for us but to stand foremost in the breach, to repair it or perish in it?

Let us concede what we ought to respect most—the collective body of the people.

My Lords, five hundred gentlemen are *not* ten millions; and, if we must first have a contention, let us take care to have the English nation on our side. If this question be given up, the freeholders of England are reduced to a condition baser than the peasantry of Poland…*unlimited power* is apt to corrupt the minds of those whom possess it, and this I know my Lords, that where law ends, there tyranny begins.

(William Pitt the Elder (1708–1798), Address to the English Parliament, January 9, 1770)

Now let us paraphrase William Pitt's argument to apply to *our* present sorry situation. When then good Senators and Representatives are all the generous efforts of *our* Forefathers, all their glorious contentions of government *by the people*, by which they meant to secure themselves and transmit to their posterity, to "We the People," a known law, a certain rule of living reduced to *this* conclusion: That instead of the arbitrary power of a king, we must submit to the arbitrary power of Congress's political party leaders. Leaders who dictate what legislation their minions may or may not support. If this be true, what benefit do we the people derive from the exchange? Tyranny, ladies and gentlemen, tyranny is detestable in every shape, but in none is it so formidable as where it is assumed and exercised by a number of tyrants, whether they call themselves Republican or Democrat. But, ladies and gentlemen, this abuse of power is a fact, but it is not a power found in *our* Constitution. We have laws, and we have a written Constitution and Bill of Rights in which every man may find the powers granted to *and restricted from use by* elected *or employed government* representatives.

It is *our* ancestors, my fellow citizens, it is to our Founding Fathers and the citizens who fought for and supported their acts that we are indebted for the laws and Constitution *we possess*. They were great and sincere, and I think that *we* have not done justice to their conduct when they took from their sovereign at the time, that great acknowledgment of individual rights contained in our Constitution and our Bill of Rights. They did not confine it to themselves alone but delivered it as a common blessing to the whole of we the people, then and now.

Now as a result of bitter animosity between these two political powers, a breach has been made in our Constitution—its battlements are dismantled, the citadel is open to the first invader, the walls totter, and the place is no longer tenable. Its strength, *the unity of the people* in support of its principles and a *mutual acceptance by us all* that all are entitled to the freedoms it provides, has been divided by the anger and revenge fostered by these political parties. Parties who seek to install *their* chosen and supported senators and representatives to positions of arbitrary power. What then remains for us but to stand foremost in the breach, to repair it or perish in it?

Let us concede what we ought to respect most—the collective body of we the people. Four hundred and thirty-five representatives and 100 senators do not represent the actual opinion of 341,814,420 citizens, and if we must first have a contention of misrepresentation, let us take care to have the American nation on our side. If this question be given up, the American voters are reduced to a condition equal to the freedoms *alleged to be exercised* by citizens of North Korea, Russia, China, Iran, and Afghanistan. Unlimited political power is apt to corrupt the minds of those who possess it, and we should know that *where the law ends, there tyranny begins.*

The Preamble of Our Constitution
of the United States of America

"We the People" of the United States, in order to form a more perfect *Union,* establish *Justice,* insure *domestic tranquility,* provide for the common defense, promote the *general Welfare,* and secure the *Blessings of Liberty,* to ourselves and our Posterity, do ordain and establish this Constitution for the United States of America."

(United States Constitution, Ratified and Adopted
by the US Congress, December 15, 1791)

Oaths of Office

President of the United States

I do solemnly swear [or affirm] that I will faithfully execute the office of President of the United States, and will to the best of my ability, preserve, protect and defend the Constitution of the United States. (Article 2, Section 1, Clause 8, United States Constitution; https:llconsttution/congress.gov)

US Congressmen and US Supreme Court Justices

I do solemnly swear [or affirm] that I will support and defend the Constitution of the United States against all enemies foreign and domestic; that I will bear true faith and allegiance to same; that I take this obligation freely, without any mental reservation or purpose of evasion; and that I well and faithfully discharge the duties of the office on which I am about to enter. So help me god. (United States Congress 1862; www.senate.gov)

US Supreme Court Justices

1789–1990

I do solemnly swear [or affirm] that I will administer justice without respect to persons, and do equal right to the poor and to the rich and I will faithfully and impartially discharge and perform all the duties incumbent upon me as a Justice of the United States Supreme Court, according to the best of my abilities and under-standing, *agreeably to the Constitution and Laws of the United States. So help me God.* (Judiciary Act of 1789, Section 8 adopted September 24, 1789)

1990–2024

I do solemnly swear [or affirm] that I will administer justice without respect to persons, and do equal right to the poor and to the rich and I will faithfully and impartially discharge and perform all the duties incumbent upon me as a Justice of the United States Supreme Court, *under the Constitution and Laws of the United States.* So help me God. (Amended by House of Representatives Judiciary Committee, December 1, 1990; Section 404 Amendment to Oath of Justices and Judges)

"Let Me Now Warn You in the Most Solemn Manner against the Baneful Effect of the Spirit of Party"

"Let me *now…warn you* in the most solemn manner against the *baneful* effects of the Spirit of Party, generally. *This spirit* unfortunately, is inseparable from our nature, having its root in the strongest passions of the human mind. It exists in all governments, more or less stifled, controlled or repressed. But in those of the popular form [those truly elective], it is seen in its greatest rankness and truly their worst enemy."

(George Washington (1732–1799), "Farewell to the Nation," September 19, 1796)

Neither the Republican nor the Democratic Parties Can Say…

Neither the Republican nor the Democratic political parties of our nation can *truly say* they are *not guilty* to some degree regarding the violent events of January 6, 2021, and the current animosity between these "parties." Their respective zealots, both of the far right and far left, have been the source of the rampant hostility, distrust, and uncompromising spirit that now permeates both parties. There is no compromise; the word is absent in their vocabularies. Their zealots have either acted violently or fostered an environment in which violence and animosity flourish. Our political leaders, *too* interested in garnering their support to win elections, have accepted their zealots' extreme politics *or*, at the least, have ignored them so as not to alienate them and lose their votes. But it has long been said that silence is approval. We, the "silent majority," have not acted to stop it either. The inability of both parties to compromise on issues, to accept the results of elections, and afterward work to achieve the goals of the winning party, and instead, acting constantly to defeat them, have compromised our system of government and are leading to its demise. Many truly independent voters have long since realized that a choice between the two current parties is a choice between the devil and the deep blue sea—both are equally dangerous. They have become the cogs in a totally dysfunctional Congress whose members have jointly striven to continue a self-fulfilling failure to govern.

We and they are supposed to be "We the People," working in concert for the good of the nation, *not* for the egos or individual goals of professional politicians. This is something our Founding Fathers never envisioned. The Founding Fathers believed that once their term in elective office was ended, our representatives would return to the general population and make room for new members with new ideas. Instead, our representatives and senators, with *"careers"* that extend for decades, lead us in a seemingly eternal conflict of "us" versus "them," blue versus red, conservative versus liberal. All this strife being wantonly led by the deemed leaders of the political parties of our nation in their baneful goals to achieve "victory" for their party. I hesitate to prefix either the words *leaders* or *political parties* with *our*, for neither are acting in *our* interest. They only strive to attain the political goals of *their* party.

Our Founding Fathers warned us that this day might come if we did not guard against it. They warned us of it before and after they had adopted and ratified our Constitution and Bill of Rights for themselves and their posterity—We the People. They foresaw that political parties were a threat to the stability and ultimate longevity of our Constitution and the tranquility of our nation. Unfortunately, it is *we* ourselves who continue this game of perpetual party politics by continuing to elect the same "established" candidates to this dysfunctional Congress. A Congress that has split our "perfect union," scoffs at our desire for "justice," threatens our "common defense," ignores our "general welfare," and, in their demeanor, fail to protect and secure *our* "Blessings of Liberty" for ourselves and our posterity.

Parties...the Greatest Political Evil

"There is nothing which I dread so much as a division of the republic into two great parties, each arranged under its leader and concerting measures in opposition to each other. This, in my humble apprehension, is the greatest political evil under our Constitution."

(John Adams (1735–1826), Letter to
Jonathan Jackson, October 2, 1780)

"By a Faction [Political Party], I Understand a Number of Citizens…Adversed to the Rights of Other Citizens"

"By a faction, I understand a number of citizens, whether amounting to a majority or a minority of the whole, who are united and actuated by some common impulse of *passion*, or of interest, and adverse to the rights of other citizens, or to the permanent and aggregate interest of the community."

(James Madison (1751–1836), "The Federalist Paper No. 10," November 22, 1787)

"Faction [A Political Party]… This Dangerous Vice… Have in Truth, Been the Mortal Disease under Which Popular Governments Have Everywhere Perished"

"Among the numerous advantages promised by a well-constructed *Union*, none deserves to be more accurately developed than its tendency to break and control the violence of faction. The friend of popular governments never finds himself so much alarmed for their character and fate, as when he contemplates their propensity to this dangerous vice. The instability, injustice, and confusion introduced into the public councils, have in truth, been the mortal diseases under which popular governments have everywhere perished."

(James Madison (1751–1836), "The Federalist Paper No. 10," November 22, 1787)

"Party...the Last Degradation
of a Free and Moral Agent"

"I have never submitted the whole system of my opinions to the creed of any party of men whatsoever, in Religion, in philosophy, in Politics or in anything else where I was capable of thinking for myself. Such an addiction is the last degradation of a free and moral agent. If I could go to heaven but with a political party, I would decline to go."

(Thomas Jefferson (1743–1826); Letter
to Francis Hopkinson, 1789)

"Parties…Hope to Evince the Justice of Their Opinions…By the Bitterness of Their Invectives"

"To judge from the conduct of the opposite Parties, we shall be led to conclude that they will mutually hope to evince the justness of their opinions, and to increase the number of their converts by the loudness of their declamations and the bitterness of their invectives."

(Alexander Hamilton (1755–1804), "The Federalist Paper No. 1," October 27, 1787)

"Intolerant Spirit…Has at All Times
Characterized Political Parties"

"Were there not even these inducements to moderation, nothing could be more ill-judged than that intolerant spirit, which has, at all times, characterized political Parties. For in politics, as in religion, it is equally absurd to aim at making proselytes by fire and sword. Heresies can rarely be cured by persecution."

(Alexander Hamilton (1755–1804), "The Federalist Paper No. 1," October 27, 1787)

"The Public Good Is Disregarded in the Conflicts of Rival Parties"

"Complaints are everywhere heard from our most considerate and virtuous citizens, equally the friends of public and private faith, and of public and personal liberty, that our governments are too unstable, that the public good is disregarded in the conflicts of rival Parties, and that measures are too often decided, not according to the rules of justice, and the Rights of the minor party, but by the superior force of an interested and overbearing majority... Our heaviest misfortunes...increasing distrust of public engagements and alarm for private Rights...must be chiefly, if not wholly, effects of the unsteadiness and injustice with which a factious spirit has tainted our public administrations."

(James Madison (1751–1836), "The Federalist Paper No. 10," November 22, 1787)

"Distrust Naturally Creates Distrust"

"Distrust naturally creates distrust, and by nothing is good-will and kind conduct more speedily changed than by invidious jealousies and uncandid imputations whether expressed or implied."

(John Jay (1745–1829), "Federalist Paper No. 5," November 10, 1787)

"We Countenance Political Intolerance"

"Bear in mind this *sacred principle*, that though the will of the majority is in all cases to prevail, that will to be rightful must be reasonable; that the minority possess their equal rights, which equal laws must protect, and to violate would be oppression.

Let us then, fellow citizens, unite with one heart and one mind. Let us restore to social intercourse that harmony and affection without which liberty and even life itself are but dreary things. And let us reflect, that having banished from our land that religious intolerance under which mankind so long bled and suffered we have gained little, if we countenance a Political intolerance, as despotic, as wicked, and as capable of as bitter and bloody persecutions…

Every difference of opinion is not a difference of principle. We have called by different names brethren of the same principle. We all are republicans; we are all federalists. If there be any among us who would wish to dissolve this Union or to change its republican form, let them stand undisturbed as monuments of the safety with which error of opinion may be tolerated, where reason is left free to combat it."

(Thomas Jefferson (1743–1804), "First
Inaugural Address," March 4, 1801)

"Beware of an Obstinate Adherence to Party"

"Every man is bound to answer these questions to himself, according to the best of his conscience and understanding, and to act agreeably to the genuine and sober dictates of his judgment. This is a duty from which nothing can give him a dispensation. 'Tis one that he is called upon. Nay, constrained by all obligations that form Bands of society, to discharge sincerely and honestly. No partial motive, no particular interest, no pride of opinion, no temporary passion or prejudice, will justify to himself, to his country, or to his posterity, an improper election of the part he is to act. Let him beware of an obstinate adherence to *party*; let him reflect that the object upon which he is to decide is not a particular interest of the community, but the very existence of the nation..."

(Alexander Hamilton (1755–1804); "The Federalist
Paper No. 85," August 13 and 16, 1788)

"Factions Act to Replace the Will of the Nation with the Will of a Party"

"The very idea of the power and the right of the people to establish Government presupposes the duty of every individual to obey the established Government [Our Constitution].

All obstructions to the execution of the Laws, all combinations or Associations [political parties], under whatever plausible character, with the real design to direct, control, counteract, or awe the regular deliberation and action of the Constituted authorities are destructive of this fundamental principal and of fatal tendency. They serve to organize Faction [political parties], to give it an artificial and extraordinary force, to put in the place of the delegated will of the Nation, the will of a Party; often a small but artful and enterprising minority of the community; and, according to the alternate triumphs of the different parties; to make the public administration the Mirror of ill concerted and incongruous projects of faction, rather than the organ of consistent and wholesome plans digested by common councils and modified by mutual interests."

(George Washington (1732–1799), "Farewell to the Nation," September 19, 1796)

"The Alternate Domination of One Faction over Another… Is Itself a Frightful Despotism"

"The alternate domination of one Faction [party] over another, sharpened by the spirit of revenge natural to Party dissension, which in different ages & countries has perpetrated the most horrid enormities, is itself a frightful despotism."

(George Washington (1732–1799), "Farewell to the Nation," September 19, 1796)

"Parties…Become Potent Engines By Which Cunning, Ambitious and Unprincipled Men…Usurp for Themselves the Reins of Government"

"However combinations or Associations of the above description may now and then answer popular ends, they are likely, in the course of time and things, to become potent engines, by which cunning, ambitious and unprincipled men will be enabled to subvert the power of the people & to usurp for themselves the reins of Government; destroying afterwards the very engines which have lifted them to unjust dominion."

(George Washington (1732–1799), "Farewell to the Nation," September 19, 1796)

"The Disorders and Miseries…
Gradually Incline the Minds of Men to Seek Security & Repose in the Absolute Power of an Individual…on the Ruins of Public Liberty"

"But this leads at length to a more formal and permanent despotism. The disorders and miseries, which result, gradually incline the minds of men to seek security & repose in the absolute power of an individual; and sooner or later the chief of some prevailing faction [party] more able or more fortunate than his competitors, turns this disposition to the purposes of his own elevation, on the ruins of Public Liberty. Without looking forward to an extremity of this kind (which nonetheless ought not be entirely out of sight) the common & continual mischiefs of the spirit of Party are sufficient to make it in the interest and duty of a wise people to discourage and restrain it."

(George Washington (1732–1799), Farewell
to the Nation, September 19, 1776)

"A Fondness for Power Is Implanted in Most Men"

"A fondness for power is implanted in most men, and it is natural to abuse it when acquired."

(Alexander Hamilton (1755–1804), *The Farmer Refuted*, February 23, 1775)

"To Consolidate the Powers of All the Departments in One…a Real Despotism"

"The spirit of encroachment tends to consolidate the powers of all the departments in one, and thus create, in whatever the form of government, a real despotism. A just estimate of that love of power, and proneness to abuse it which predominates in the human heart, is sufficient to satisfy us on the truth of this position."

(George Washington (1732–1799), "Farewell to the Nation," September 19, 1796)

"The Idea of [Political Parties] Introducing a Monarchy or Aristocracy [or Dictatorship] into This Country Is One of Those Visionary Things That None but Madmen Could Meditate"

"The idea of introducing a monarchy or aristocracy in this Country, by employing the influence and force of a Government continually changing hands towards it, *is* one of those visionary things, that none but madmen would meditate and that no wise men would believe."

(Alexander Hamilton (1755–1804), "Objections and Answers Respecting the Administration," August 18, 1792)

"A People…of This Country… Can Surely Never Be Brought to It, but from…the Acts of Popular Demagogues"

"To hope the people may be cajoled into giving their sanctions to such institutions is still more chimerical. A people so enlightened and so diversified as the people of this Country can surely never be brought to it, but from convulsions and disorders in consequence of the acts of popular demagogues."

(Alexander Hamilton (1755–1804), "Objections and Answers Respecting the Administration," August 18, 1792)

"Men of Factious Tempers…Betray the Interests of the People"

"Men of factious tempers, of local prejudices, or of sinister design, may, by intrigue, by corruption or by other means, first obtain the suffrages, and then betray the interests, of the people."

(James Madison (1751–1836), "The Federalist Paper No. 10," November 22, 1787)

"An Enlightened Zeal
for the Energy and Efficiency of Government
Will Be Stigmatized as the Offspring of
a Temper Fond of Despotic Power"

"An enlightened zeal for the energy and efficiency of government will be stigmatized as the offspring of a temper fond of despotic power and hostile to the principles of liberty. An over scrupulous jealousy of danger to the rights of the people, which is more commonly the fault of the head than the heart will be represented as mere pretense and artifice, the stale bail for popularity at the expense of public good."

(Alexander Hamilton (1755–1804), "The Federalist Paper No. 1," October 27, 1787)

"The Spirit of Party…Foments Occasionally Riot & Insurrection"

"The spirit of party…serves to distract the Public Councils and enfeeble the Public Administration. It agitates the community with ill founded jealousies and false alarms, kindles the animosity of one part against another, foments occasionally riot & insurrection. It opens the door to foreign influence & corruption, which find a facilitated access to government itself through the channels of party passions. Thus the policy and will of one country, are subjected to the policy and will of another."

(George Washington (1732–1799), "Farewell to the Nation," 1796)

"The Truth Is…the Only Path to a Subversion of the Republican System of the Country Is…to Throw Affairs into Confusion"

"The truth unquestionably is, that the only path to a subversion of the republican system of the Country is, by flattering the prejudices of the people, and exciting their jealousies and apprehensions, to throw affairs into confusion, and bringing on civil commotion. Tired at length of anarchy or want of government, they may take shelter in the arm of monarchy [rule by one person] for repose and security."

(Alexander Hamilton (1755–1804), "Objections and Answers Respecting the Administration," August 18, 1792)

"Those Then, Who Resist a Confirmation of Public Order May Justly Be Suspected…to Throw Things into Confusion That He May Ride the Storm and Direct the Wind"

"Those then, who resist a confirmation of public order, *are* the true Artificers on monarchy *[Rule by One Person]* not that this is the intention of the generality of them. Yet it would <u>not</u> be difficult to lay the finger upon some of *their party* who may justly be suspected.

When a man unprincipled in private life, desperate in his fortune, bold in his temper, possessed of considerable talents, having the advantage of Military habits—despotic in his ordinary demeanor—known to have scoffed in private at the principles of liberty—when such a man is seen to mount the hobby horse of popularity—to join in the cry of danger to liberty—to take every opportunity of embarrassing the General Government & bringing it under suspicion—to flatter and fall in with all the non sense of the zealots of the day—it may justly be suspected that his object is to throw things into confusion that he may "ride the storm and direct the wind."

(Alexander Hamilton (1755–1804), "Objections and Answers Respecting the Administration," August 18, 1792)

"Insurrection...Eventually Endangers All Government"

"An insurrection *whatever* may be its immediate cause, eventually endangers *all* government."

(Alexander Hamilton (1755–1804), "Federalist Paper No. 28," December 16, 1787)

"A Firm Union Will Be...
as a Barrier Against
Domestic Faction and Insurrection...
Sedition and Party Rage"

"A firm union [of We the People] will be of the utmost moment to the peace and liberty of the States, as a barrier against domestic faction and insurrection... If now and then intervals of felicity open themselves to view, we behold them with a mixture of regret, arising from the reflection that the pleasing scenes before us are soon to be overwhelmed by the tempestuous waves of sedition and party rage."

(Alexander Hamilton (1755–1804), "The Federalist Paper No. 9," November 21, 1787)

The Spirit of Party "Demands a Uniform Vigilance to Prevent Its Bursting into a Flame, Lest Instead of Warming It Should Consume"

"There is an opinion that parties in free countries are useful checks upon the Administration of the Government and serve to keep alive the spirit of liberty. This within certain limits is probably true—and in Governments of a Monarchical cast Patriotism may look with indulgence, if not favor, upon the spirit of party. But in those of popular character, in Governments purely elective, it is a spirit not to be encouraged. From their natural tendency, it is certain there will always be enough of that spirit for every salutary purpose. And, there being constant danger of excess the effort ought to be, by force of public opinion, to mitigate & assuage it. A fire not to be quenched, it demands a uniform vigilance to prevent its bursting into a flame, lest instead of warming it should consume."

(George Washington (1732–1799), "Farewell to the Nation," 1796)

These Warnings Are Intended
to "Moderate the Fury of Party Spirit"

"In offering to you, my Countrymen, these counsels of an old and affectionate friend, I dare not hope they will make the strong & lasting impression, I could wish -that they will control the usual current of passions, or prevent our Nation from running the course which has hitherto marked the Destiny of Nations; But if I may flatter myself, that they might be productive of some partial benefit, some occasional good, that they may now and then recur to moderate the fury of party spirit, to warn against the mischiefs of foreign intrigue, to guard against the Impostures of pretended patriotism - this hope will be full recompense for the solicitude for your welfare, by which they have been dictated."

(George Washington (1732–1799), "Farewell
to the Nation," September 19, 1796)

"A Man under the Tyranny of Party Spirit is the Greatest Slave upon Earth, for None but Himself Can Deprive Him of Freedom of Thought"

"When men have rashly plunged themselves into a measure, the right or wrong of it is soon forgotten. Party knows no impulse but spirit, no prize but victory. It is blind to truth, and hardened against conviction. It seeks to justify error by perseverance, and denies to its own mind the operation of its own judgment. A man under the tyranny of party spirit is the greatest slave upon earth, for no one but himself can deprive him of the freedom of thought."

(Thomas Paine (1737–1809), "Opposers
to the Bank," March 7, 1787)

"As Nations Become Corrupt and Vicious
They Have More Need for Masters"

"Only a virtuous people are capable of freedom. As nations become corrupt and vicious they have more need for masters."

(Benjamin Franklin (1706–1790), "Letters to Messrs, the Abbes Chalut and Arnaud," April 17, 1787)

"This Constitution…Is Likely to Be Well Administered for a Course of Years, and Can Only End in Despotism as Other Forms Have Done Before, When the People Shall Become So Corrupted as to Need Despotic Government, Being Incapable of Any Other"

"In these sentiments, Sir, I agree to this Constitution, with all its faults, if they are such; because I think a General Government necessary for us, and there is no form of Government but what may be a Blessing to the People if well administered; and I believe farther that this is likely to be well administered for a Course of Years, and can ONLY end in Despotism as other Forms have done before, when the people shall become so corrupted as to need Despotic Government, being incapable of any other."

(Benjamin Franklin (1706–1790), "Speech in Convention," September 17, 1787)

"We the People"

We the people have allowed our so-called *leaders* to stray from the processes which have insured that *our* system of government will work to *our* benefit. They are three in number and are called *toleration*, *compromise*, and *common sense*. Our government has not continued to exist because one party or the other imposed its ideas as the *only* true and correct direction to proceed on any matter, that those who vary from their point of view are to be considered an enemy and belittled and derided, disenfranchised. Truly, it must be admitted *that* our political leaders are "professional politicians," often appearing more interested in keeping their prestigious congressional positions than actually legislating. They have led us down a path where it is assumed that because one wins an election, one's goals are to be blindly accepted as the goals of all, and *that* any opposing views can be wantonly disregarded and blatantly hidden behind the lip service spouted by both parties of purportedly representing both sides of the aisle. When such lies are promoted and found to be merely political rhetoric and the desires, views, and concerns of the minority are ignored or belittled, it fosters resentment and hostility—*alas!*—the description of our current political and social environment. Their eternal bickering with each other gives justification to the belief that we as a people *cannot* govern ourselves. That democracy, which we all profess to cherish, is not functional. But the problem at its basics lies with *We the People*. When we allow ourselves to be led like unthinking sheep by political advertising which demonizes opponents and heaps unmitigated praise upon he who pays the bill, we throw away our own power to make change. Think not as a Republican or Democrat but as an American. The "political machines" that generate these ads are *not* out to promote truth, but merely to succeed in raising *their* candidate and his or her minions to power. It will take all of us to put our political parties in their place—not as self-indulgent politicians but as *obedient* servants of *We the People*.

One would think that the aforementioned warnings, particularly those given to us by our First President upon leaving office, might be of interest to our past and present political leaders. For numerous years, Washington's Farewell Address was read yearly in the chambers of both our Senate and House of Representatives on the celebration of his birthday, recurring to remind our representatives of the dangers he spoke of. In 1979, forty-five years ago, our House of Representatives discontinued this tradition, and though the Senate has retained it, the question is whether the senators present for its reading actually listen to and grasp that the warnings apply to them, or that though it is spoken, it is *not heard*. It is a sad day indeed when their love of *party*, Republican or Democrat, and desire for *personal aggrandizement*, supplants their love of country.

We the People Must Hold All Our Elected Representatives Accountable to Our Constitution and Laws *and We the People*

Remember, our duly elected Senators and Representatives are merely men and women to whom *we* have delegated legislative (lawmaking) powers. But, once they have garnered our votes, and with the support of *their* party, *their* personal beliefs, prejudices, and desire for even *more* political power and prestige and *their* allegiance to *their* "party" often influence their decisions and votes. Votes that should be for the good of We the People become votes to advance the positions supported *by the party "leaders"* and adverse to their opponents' positions, often arbitrary and partisan acts not necessarily for the good of We the People.

We, as the voters, elevate these men and women into positions of power, which are all too often abused and misused to settle personal and political grievances and desires, with reputedly learned men and women reverting to self-righteous tirades against anyone who disagrees with *their* sanctimonious opinions. Because of this *anger*, perpetuated by derogatory sentiments expressed by *both* sides, some of our elected representatives are seemingly driven more by the "revenge" referred to by President Washington than by a desire to legislate. Indeed, many of We the People ourselves have adopted this feeling of revenge and gravitate toward those representatives who appeal to our fears, willing to sacrifice *our* freedoms and rights to placate *our* anger.

Our elected representatives are failing to carry out the important duties to which they were assigned. Do they truly represent us? Their allegiance is tied *too tightly to their respective party and their respective Congressional leaders*. They have abandoned the primary tool of legislating in a democracy—compromise. They have chosen, rather, to attempt to arbitrarily impose their opinions and, when prohibited from doing so, to hamper and impede the passage of legislation. It is up to us, the silent majority, to silence the acrimonious contentions of such radical party zealots, both to the left and right, with our votes and voices. We must hold *all* of our elected representatives accountable to our Constitution and our laws and to We the People, to whom their only true and valid allegiance lies. They apparently refuse to do this on their own. *We must* return the concepts of toleration, compromise, and common sense to our government.

"They Find Us…Destitute of an Effectual Government"

"But whatever may be our situation, whether firmly united under one national government, or split into a number of confederacies, certain it is that foreign nations will know and view it exactly as is; and they will act toward us accordingly. If they see that our national government is efficient and well administered, our people free, our trade prudently regulated, our militia properly organized and disciplined, our resources and finances discreetly managed, our credit reestablished, our people free, contented and united, they will be much more disposed to cultivate friendship than to provoke resentment. If, on the other hand, they find us either destitute of an effectual government (each state doing right or wrong, as to its rulers may seem convenient), or three or four independent and probably discordant republics or confederacies, one inclining to Britain, another to France, and a third to Spain, and perhaps played off against each other by the three, what a poor pitiful figure will America make in their eyes! How liable would she become not only to their contempt but to their outrage, and how soon would dear bought experience proclaim that when a people or family so divide, it never fails to be against themselves.

(John Jay (1745–1829), "Federalist No. 4," November 7, 1777)

"Weakness and Divisions at Home... Invite Dangers from Abroad"

"To the People of the State of New York:

Queen Anne, in her letter of the 1st July, 1706, to the Scotch Parliament, makes some observations on the importance of the UNION then forming between England and Scotland, which merit our attention. I shall present the public with one or two extracts from it: 'An entire and perfect union will be the solid foundation of lasting peace: It will secure your religion, liberty, and property; remove the animosities amongst yourselves, and the jealousies and differences betwixt our two kingdoms. It must increase your strength, riches, and trade; and by this union the whole island, being joined in affection and free from all apprehension of different interest, will be enabled to resist all its enemies. We most earnestly recommend to you calmness and unanimity in this great and weighty affair, that the union may be brought to a happy conclusion, being the only effectual way to secure present and future happiness, and disappoint the designs of our and your enemies, who will doubtless, on this occasion, use their utmost endeavors to prevent or delay this union.'

It was remarked in the preceding paper, that weakness and division at home would invite dangers from abroad and that nothing would tend more to secure us from them than union, strength, and good government within ourselves. This subject is copious and cannot easily be exhausted.

The history of Great Britain is the one with which we are in general the best acquainted, and it gives us many useful lessons. We may profit from their experience without paying the price it costs them. Although it seems obvious to common sense that the people of such an island should be but one nation, yet we find that they were for many ages divided into three and that those three were almost constantly embroiled in quarrels and wars with one another. Notwithstanding their true interest with respect to the continental nations was really the same, yet by the arts and policy and practices of those nations, their mutual, jealousies were perpetually kept inflamed, and for a long series of years, they were far more inconvenient and troublesome than they were useful and assisting to each other.

Should the people of America divide themselves into three or four nations, would not the same thing happen? Would not similar jealousies arise, and be in like manner cherished? Instead of their being "joined in affection" and free from all apprehension of different "interests" envy and jealousy would soon extinguish confidence and affection, and the partial interests of each confederacy, instead of the general interests of all America, would be the only objects of their policy and pursuits. Hence, like most other BORDERING nations, they would always be either involved in disputes and war, or live in the constant apprehension of them.

The most sanguine advocates of three or four confederacies cannot reasonably suppose that they would long remain exactly on an equal footing in point of strength, even if it was possible to form them so at first; but admitting that to be practicable, yet what human contrivance can secure the continuance of such equality? Independent of those local circumstances which tend to beget and increase power in one part and to impede progress in another, we must advert to the effects of that superior policy and good management which would probably distinguish the government on one above the rest, and by which their relative equality in strength and consideration would be destroyed. For it cannot be presumed that the same degree of sound policy, prudence, and foresight would uniformly be observed by each of these confederacies for a long succession of years.

Whenever, and from whatever causes, it might happen, and happen it would, that any one of these nations or confederacies should rise on the scale of political importance much above the degree of her neighbors, that moment would those neighbors behold her with envy and with fear. Both those passions would lead them to countenance, if not to promote, whatever might promise to diminish her importance; and would also restrain them from measures calculated to advance or even to secure her prosperity. Much time would not be necessary to enable her to discern these unfriendly dispositions. He would soon begin not only to lose confidence in her neighbors but also to feel a disposition equally unfavorable to them. Distrust naturally creates distrust, and by nothing is goodwill and kind conduct more speedily changed than by invidious jealousies and uncandid imputations, whether expressed or implied.

The North is generally the region of strength, and many local circumstances render it probable that the most Northern of the proposed confederacies would, at a period of time not very distant, be unquestionably more formidable than any of the others. No sooner would this become evident than the *NORTHERN HIVE* would excite the same ideas and sensations in the more southern parts of America which it formerly did in the southern parts of Europe. Nor does it appear to be a rash conjecture that its young swarms might often be tempted to gather honey in the more blooming fields and milder air of their luxurious and more delicate neighbors.

They who well consider the history of similar divisions and confederacies will find abundant reason to apprehend that those in contemplation would in no other sense be neighbors as they would be borderers; that they would neither love nor trust one another, but on the contrary would be a prey to discord, jealousy and mutual injuries; in short, that they would place us exactly in the situations in which some nations doubtless wish to see us, viz., *formidable only to each other.*

From these considerations it appears that those gentlemen are greatly mistaken who suppose that alliances offensive and defensive might be formed between these confederacies, and would produce that combination and union of wills of arms and of resources, which would be necessary to put and keep them in a formidable state of defense against foreign enemies.

When did the independent states, into which Britain, and Spain were formerly divided, combined in such alliance, or unite their forces against a foreign enemy? The proposed confederacies will be DISTINCT NATIONS. Each of them would have its commerce with foreigners to regulate by distinct treaties; and as their productions and commodities are different and proper for different markets, so would those treaties be essentially different. Different commercial concerns must create different interests, and of course different degrees of political attachment to and connection with foreign nations. Hence it might and probably will happen that the foreign nation with whom the SOUTHERN confederacy might be at war would be the one with whom the NORTHERN confederacy would be the most desirous of preserving peace and friendship. An alliance so contrary to their immediate interest would not therefore be easy to form, nor, if formed, would it be observed and fulfilled with perfect good faith.

Nay, it is far more probable that in America, as in Europe, neighboring nations, acting under the impulse of opposite interests and unfriendly passions, would frequently be found taking different sides. Considering our distance from Europe, it would be more natural for these confederacies to apprehend danger from one another than from distant nations, and therefore, each of them should be more desirous to guard against the others by the aid of foreign alliances than to guard against foreign dangers by alliances between themselves. And let us not forget how much more easy it is to receive foreign fleets into our ports and foreign armies into our country than it is to persuade or compel them to depart. How many conquests did the Romans and others make in the character of allies, and what innovations did they under the same character introduce into the governments of those whom they pretended to protect?

Let candid men judge, then, whether the division of America into any given number of independent sovereignties would tend to secure us against the hostilities and improper interference of foreign nations."

(John Jay (1745–1829), "Federalist Letter
No. 5," November 10, 1777)

Have Our "Party" Leaders Led Us to the Point Mr. Jefferson Warned Us of as Early as 1781?

"From the conclusion of this war [Our Revolutionary War] we shall be going downhill. It will not then be necessary to resort every moment to the people for support. They [We the People] will be forgotten therefore [by government & our elected representatives], and their [We the People's] Rights disregarded. They [We] will forget themselves [ourselves], but in the sole faculty of making money, and, will never think of uniting to effect a due respect for their [our] Rights. The shackles [the threat of government infringement of our civil rights] therefore, which shall not be knocked off at the conclusion of this war, *will remain on us long*, will be made heavier and heavier till our Rights shall be revived or expire in a convulsion."

(Thomas Jefferson (1743–1826), "Notes on the State of Virginia," 1781)

Or Are We Now Content to Do
What Mr. Benjamin Franklin
Warned Us of as Early as 1759?

"Those who would give up essential liberty, to purchase a little temporary safety, deserve neither liberty or safety."

(Benjamin Franklin (1706–1790) and Richard Jackson (1721–1787), "A Historical Review of the Constitutional Government of Pennsylvania from its Origin," 1759)

"Our Calamity Is Heightened by Reflecting That We Furnish the Means by Which We Suffer"

"Society, in every state is a blessing. Government even in its best state, is but a necessary evil; For, when we suffer or are exposed to the same miseries by a government which we might expect from a country without government, our calamity is heightened by reflecting that *we* furnish the means by which we suffer."

(Thomas Paine (1737–1809), "Common Sense," February 14, 1776)

"Posterity!…Freedom…I Hope You Make Good Use of It"

"Posterity! You will never know how much it cost the present generation to preserve your freedom. I hope you will make good use of it! If you do not I shall repent in heaven that I ever took half the pains to preserve it."

(John Adams (1735–1826), "Letter to Abigail Adams," August 26, 1877)

"If Destruction Be Our Lot,
We Must Ourselves Be Its Author and Finisher. As a Nation of Freemen, We Must Live through All Time, or Die by Suicide."

(Forty-Seven Years Later 1791–1838
President Washington's Warnings Revisited

On January 27, 1838, 185 years ago, 50 years after the ratification of our Constitution, 47 years after the ratification of our Bill of Rights, 47 years after Washington's Farewell Address, and 23 years before our Civil War, Abraham Lincoln had cause to remind us of the threat to our nation that we ourselves pose if we are not united. He would revisit Washington's warnings to us. We did not listen then, and the result was a Civil War that tore OUR nation apart, ending the lives of roughly 750,000 citizens. Read on, and you can see THAT what he said in 1838 is equally applicable to our society TODAY.

Lincoln's Lyceum Address
Springfield, Illinois, January 27, 1838

As a subject for the remarks of the evening, "The perpetuation of our political institutions" is selected.

In the great journal of things happening under the sun, we the American People, find our account running, under date of the nineteenth century of the Christian era. We find ourselves in the peaceful possession, of the fairest portion of the earth, as regards extent of territory, fertility of soil, and salubrity of climate.

We find ourselves under the government of a system of political institutions, conducing more essentially to the ends of civil and religious liberty, than any of which the history of former times tells us.

We, when mounting the stage of existence, found ourselves the legal inheritors of these fundamental blessings. We toiled not in the acquirement or establishment of them, they are a legacy bequeathed us, by a once hardy, brave, and patriotic, but *now* lamented and departed race of ancestors. Theirs' was the task (and nobly they performed it) to possess themselves, and through themselves to us, of this goodly land; and to uprear upon it hills and its valleys a political edifice of liberty and equal rights.

"Tis ours only, to transmit these, the former unprofaned by the foot of an invader"; the latter, undecayed by the lapse of time and untorn by usurpation, to the latest generation that fate shall permit the world to know. This task of gratitude to our fathers, justice to ourselves, duty to posterity, and love for our species in general, all imperatively require us faithfully to perform.

How then shall we perform it? At what point shall we expect the approach of danger?

By what means shall we fortify against it? Shall we expect some transatlantic military giant, to step the Ocean, and crush us at a blow? *Never!* All the armies of Europe, Asia and Africa combined, with all the treasure of the earth (our own excepted) in their military chest; with a Bounaparte for a commander, could not by force take a drink from the Ohio, or make attack on the Blue Ridge, in a trial of a thousand years.

At what point then is the approach of danger to be expected? I answer, if it ever reach us, it must spring up amongst us. It cannot come from abroad. If destruction be our lot, we must ourselves be its author and finisher. As a nation of freemen, we must live through all time, or die by suicide. I hope I am over wary, but if I am not, *there is, even now, something of ill omen amongst us…the increasing disregard for law which pervades the country; the growing disposition to substitute the wild and furious passions; in lieu of the sober judgment of courts; and the worse than savage mobs, for the executive ministers of justice.*

This disposition is awfully fearful in any community; and that it now exists in ours, though grating to our feelings to admit, it would be a violation of truth, and an insult to our intelligence to deny it.

Accounts of outrages committed by mobs, form the every-day news of the times. They have pervaded the country, from New England to Louisiana; they are neither peculiar to the eternal snows of the former, nor the burning suns of the latter; they are not the creature of climate; neither are they confined to the slave-holding, or to non-slave-holding States. Alike, they spring up among the pleasure hunting masters of Southern slaves, and the order loving citizens of the land of steady habits. Whatever, then, their cause may be, it is common to the whole Country.

It would be tedious, as well as useless, to recount the horrors of all of them. Those happening in the State of Mississippi, and at St. Louis, are, perhaps the most dangerous in example, and revolting to humanity. In the Mississippi case, they FIRST commenced by hanging the regular gamblers; a set of men, certainly not following for a livelihood, a very useful, or very honest occupation; but one which, so far from being forbidden by the laws, was actually licensed by an act of the legislature, passed but a single year before.

Next, negroes, suspected of conspiring to raise an insurrection, were caught up and hanged in all parts of the State; Then, white men, supposed to be leagued with the negroes; and finally strangers, from neighboring States, going thither on business, were, in many instances subjected to the same fate.

Thus went on this process of hanging, from gamblers to negroes, from negroes to white citizens, and from these to strangers; till dead men were seen literally dangling from the boughs of trees upon every roadside; and in numbers almost sufficient, to rival the native Spanish moss of the country, as a drapery of the forest.

Turn, then, to that horror-striking scene at St. Louis. A single victim was only sacrificed there. His story is very short; and is, perhaps, the most highly tragic, if anything of its length, that has ever been witnessed in real life. A mulatto man, by the name of McIntosh, was seized in the street, dragged to the suburbs of the city, chained to a tree, and actually burned to death; and all within a single hour from the time he had been a freeman, attending to his own business, and at peace with the world.

Such are the effects of mob law; and such as the scenes, becoming more and more frequent in this land so lately famed for love of law and order; and the stories of which, have even now grown TOO familiar, to attract anything more, than an idle remark.

*"What has this to do with the perpetuation
of our political institutions?"*

But you are, perhaps, ready to ask, "What has this to do with the perpetuation of our political institutions?" I answer, it has much to do with it. Its direct consequences are, comparatively speaking, but a small evil; and much of its danger consists, in the proneness of our minds, to regard its direct, as its only consequences. Abstractly considered, the hanging of the gamblers at Vicksburg, was of but little consequence. They constitute a portion of the population, that is worse than useless in a community; and their death, if no pernicious example be set by it, is never a matter of reasonable regret with anyone. If they were annually swept, from the stage of existence, by the plague or small pox, honest men would, perhaps, be much profited, by the operation.

Similarly too, is the correct reasoning, in regard to the burning on the negro at St. Louis. He had forfeited his life, by the perpetration of an outrageous murder upon one of the most worthy and respectable citizens of the city; and had he not died as he did, he must have died by the sentence of the law, in a very short time afterwards. As to him alone, it was as well the way it otherwise have been.

"The Full Extent of the Evil"

But the example in either case, was fearful. When men take it in their heads, to hang gamblers, or burn murderers, they should recollect, that, in the confusion usually attending such transactions, they will be as likely to hang or burn someone who is neither a gambler nor a murderer as one who is; And that, acting upon the example they set, the mob of tomorrow, may, and probably will, hang or burn some of them by the very same mistake. And not only so; the innocent, those who have ever set their faces against violations of the law in every shape, alike with the guilty, fall victims to the ravages of mob law; and thus it goes on, step by step, till the walls erected for the defense of the persons and property of individuals, are trodden down and disregarded. *But all this even, is not the full extent of the evil.*

By such examples, by instances of the perpetrators of such acts going unpunished, the lawless in spirit, are encouraged to become lawless in practice; and having been used to no restraint, but dread of punishment, they thus become absolutely unrestrained.

Having ever regarded Government as their deadliest bane, they make jubilee of the suspension of its operations; and pray for nothing so much, as its total annihilation.

While, on the other hand, good men, men who love tranquility, whom desire to abide by the law, and enjoy their benefits, who would gladly spill their blood in defense of their country, seeing their property destroyed; their families insulted, and their lives endangered; their persons injured; and seeing nothing in prospect that forebodes a change for the better, become tired of, and disgusted with, a Government which offers them no protection; and are not so much adverse to a change in which they imagine they have nothing to lose.

"The strongest bulwark of any government...
[the attachment of the people]...

Thus, then, by the operation of this mobocratic spirit, which all must admit, is now abroad in the land, the strongest bulwark of any Government, and particularly of those constituted like ours, may effectively be broken down and destroyed. - I mean the attachment of the people. Whenever this effect shall be produced among us; whenever the vicious portion of the population shall be permitted to gather in bands of hundreds and thousands, and burn churches, ravage and rob provision stores, throw printing presses into rivers, shoot editors, and hang and burn obnoxious persons at pleasure, and with impunity, depend on it, this government cannot last. By such things, the feelings of the best citizens will become more of less alienated from it; and thus it will be left without friends, or with too few, and those few too weak, to make their friendship effectual.

[A Threat to Our Constitution
from the Rise of a Demagogue]

At such time and under such circumstances, men of sufficient talent and ambition will not be wanting to seize the opportunity, strike the blow, and overturn that fair fabric, which for the last half century, has been the fondest hope, of the lovers of freedom, throughout the world.

I know the American People are much attached to their Government; I know they would suffer much for its sake; I know they would endure evils long and patiently; before they would ever think of exchanging it for another. Yet, notwithstanding all this, if the laws be continually despised and disregarded, if their rights to be secure in their persons and property, are held by no better tenure than the caprice of a mob, the alienation of their affections from the Government is the natural consequence; and to that, sooner or later, it must come. Here then, is one point at which danger may be expected.

"How Shall We Fortify against It?"

The questions recurs, "how shall we fortify against it?" The answer is simple. Let every American, every lover of liberty, every well wisher to his posterity, swear by the blood of the revolution, never to violate in the least particular, the laws of the country; and never to tolerate their violation by others. As the patriots of seventy-six did to support of the Declaration of Independence, so to the support of the Constitution and Laws, let every American pledge his life, his property, and his sacred honor; let every man remember that to violate the law, is to trample on the blood of his father; and to tear the character of his own and his children's liberty. Let reverence for the laws, be breathed by every American mother, to the lisping babe, that prattles on her lap; let it be taught in schools, in seminaries, and in colleges; let it be written in Primers, spelling books, and in Almanacs; Let it be preached from the pulpit, proclaimed in legislative halls, and enforced in courts of justice. And, in short, let it become the political religion of the nation; and let the old and the young, the rich and the poor, the grave and the gay, of all sexes and tongues, and colors and conditions, sacrifice unceasingly upon its altars. While ever a state of feeling such as this, shall universally, or even very generally prevail throughout the nation, vain will be every effort, and fruitless every attempt, to subvert our national freedom.

When I so pressingly urge a strict observance of ALL the laws. let me not be understood as saying there are no bad laws, nor that grievances may not arise, for the redress of which, no legal provisions have been made, I mean to say no such thing. But I do mean to say, that, although bad laws, if they exist, should be repealed as soon as possible, still while they continue in force, for the sake of example, they should be religiously observed. So also, in unprovided cases. If such arise, let proper legal provisions be made for them with the least possible delay; BUT, till then, if not too intolerable, be borne with.

"There is no grievance that is the fit object
of redress by mob law"

There is NO grievance that is a fit object of redress by mob law. In any case that arises as for instance, the promulgation of abolitionism, one of two positions is necessarily true; That is, the thing is right within itself; and therefore deserves the protection of all law and all good citizens; or, it is wrong, and therefore proper to be prohibited by legal enactments; and in neither case, is the interposition of mob law, either necessary, justifiable, or excusable.

But, it may be asked, why suppose danger to our political institutions? Have we not preserved them for more than fifty years? And why may we not for fifty times as long?

We hope there is no sufficient reason. We hope all dangers may be overcome; but to conclude that no danger may ever arise, would itself be extremely dangerous. There are now, and will hereafter be, many causes, dangerous in their tendency, which have not existed heretofore; and which are not too insignificant to merit attention.

That our government should have been maintained in its original form from its establishment until now, is not much to be wondered at. It had many props to support it through that period, which now are decayed and crumbled away. Through that period, it was felt by all, to be an undecided experiment; Now, it is understood to be a successful one. Then, all that sought celebrity and fame, and distinction, expected to find them in the success of that experiment. Their all was staked upon it; Their destiny was inseparably linked with it. Their ambition aspired to display ore an admiring world, the practical demonstration of the truth of a proposition, which had hitherto been considered, at best no better, than problematical; namely, the capability of a people to govern themselves. If they succeeded, they were to be immortalized; their names were to be transferred to counties and cities, and rivers and mountains; and to be revered and sung, and toasted through all time. If they failed, they were to be called knaves and fools, and fanatics for a fleeting hour; than to sink and be forgotten. They succeeded. The experiment is successful; and thousands have won their deathless names in making it so.

[THREATS POSED BY A DEMAGOGUE]

But the game is caught; and I believe it is true, that with the catching, ends the pleasure of the chase. This field of glory is harvested, and the crop is already appropriated. But new reapers will arise, and they too, will seek a field. It is to deny, what the history of the world tells us is true, to suppose that men of ambition and talents will not continue to spring up amongst us. And when they do, they will as naturally seek the gratification of their ruling passion, as others have before them. The question then, is, can that gratification be found in supporting and maintaining an edifice that has been erected by others? Most certainly *it cannot*.

Many great and good men sufficiently qualified for any task they should undertake, may ever be found, whose ambition would inspire to nothing beyond a seat in Congress, a gubernatorial or a presidential chair; but such belong not to the family of the lion, or the tribe of the eagle. *What!* think you these places would satisfy an Alexander, a Caesar or a Napoleon? *Never!* Towering genius disdains a beaten path. It seeks regions hitherto unexplored. It seeks no distinction in adding story upon story, upon monuments of fame, erected to the memory of others. It denies that it is glory enough to serve under any chief. It scorns to tread in the footsteps of any predecessor, however illustrious. It thirst and burns for distinction; and, if possible, it will have it, whether at the expense of emancipating slaves or enslaving freemen.

It is reasonable then to expect, that some man possessed of the loftiest genius, coupled with ambition sufficient to push it to its utmost stretch, will at some time, spring up among us? And when such a one does, it will require the people to be united with each other, attached to the government and laws, and generally intelligent, to successfully frustrate his designs. Distinction will be his paramount object, and although he would as willingly, perhaps more so, acquire it by doing good as harm, yet, that opportunity being past, and nothing left to be done in the way of building up, he would set boldly to the task of pulling down. Here, then, is a probable case, highly dangerous, and such a one as could not have existed heretofore.

Another reason which once was; but which to the same extent, is now no more, has done much in maintaining our institutions thus far. I mean the powerful influence which the interesting scenes of the revolution has upon the passions of the people as distinguished from their judgment. By this influence, the jealousy, envy and avarice, incident to our nature, and so common to a state in peace, prosperity and conscious strength, were, for the time, in a great measure smothered and rendered inactive; while the deep-rooted principles of hate, and the powerful motive of revenge instead of being turned against each other, were directed exclusively against the British nation.

And thus, from the force of circumstance, the basest principles of our nature, were either made to lie dormant, or to become the active agents in the advancement of the noblest cause—that of establishing and maintaining civil and religious liberty. But this state of feeling must fade, is fading, has faded with the circumstances that produced it.

I do not mean to say, that the scenes of the revolution are now or ever will be entirely forgotten; But that like everything else, they must fade upon the memory of the world, and grow more and more dim by the lapse of time. In history, we hope, they will be read of, and recounted so long as the Bible shall be read; But even granting that they will, their influence cannot be what it heretofore has been. Even then, they cannot be so universally known, nor so vividly felt, as they were by the generation just gone to rest. At the close of that struggle, nearly every adult male had been a participator in some of its scenes. The consequence was, that of those scenes, in the form of a husband, a father, a son or brother, a living history was to be found in every family, a history bearing the indubitable testimonies of its own authenticity, in the limbs mangled, in the scars of wounds received, in the midst of the very scenes related, a history too, that could be read and understood alike by all, the wise and the ignorant, the learned and the unlearned. But those histories are gone. They can be read no more forever. They were a fortress of strength, but what invading foe and man could never do, the silent artillery of time has done, the leveling of its walls. They are gone. They were a forest of giant oaks but the all-resistless hurricane has swept over them, and left only here and there, a lonely trunk, despoiled of its verdure, shorn of its foliage; unshading and unshaded, to murmur in a few gentle breezes, and to combat with its mutilated limbs, a few more ruder storms, then to sink, and be no more.

"Passion in the future…will be our enemy"

They were the pillars of the temple of liberty, and now, that they have crumbed away, that temple must fall, unless we, their descendants supply their places with other pillars, hewn from the solid quarry of sober reason. Passion has helped us; but can do so no more. It will in the future be our enemy. Reason, cold, calculating, unimpassioned reason, must furnish all the materials for our future support and defense. Let those materials be molded into general intelligence, sound morality, and in particular, a reverence for the Constitution and laws and, that we improved to the last; that we remained free to the last; that we revered his name to the last; that during his long sleep, we permitted no hostile foot to pass over or desecrate his resting place; shall be that which is to learn the last trumpet shall awaken our Washington. Upon these let the proud fabric of freedom rest, as the rock of its basis; and as truly as has been said of the only greater institution, "the gates of hell shall not prevail against it."

(Abraham Lincoln, "Lyceum Address,"
Springfield, Illinois, January 27, 1838)
Source: *Collected Works of Abraham Lincoln*,
edited by Ror P. Basler et al.

Has Our Government in Reality Become an Aristocracy Comprised of Enriched and Pompous Professional Politicians?

The two political parties of our nation were originally founded to unite representatives of like thinking in working to pass legislation, which reflected "our" values and thinking as conveyed to them by their election. We hope that through compromise and the number of votes they could peacefully garner, to achieve that compromise for all to be successful. Over the years, it seems, this lofty goal has been forgotten, and the power and prestige of the delegated positions in the three branches of our government—Executive, Legislative, and Judicial—has corrupted many who may have entered public service with the highest and purest of aspirations to do good. But "power corrupts, and absolute power corrupts absolutely," and the absolute allegiance which the two particular parties require of their members has removed from the floor of our Congress toleration, common sense, and the ability to compromise from seemingly most if not all of our elected representatives.

Our political leaders hold that our two parties are needed for our government to function. This is only true if the members of Congress are free to act upon their consciences without being demeaned if their consciences do not agree with that of their associated "parties." Being a party member does not make the representative or senator a robotic and absolute "Republican" or "Democrat" tied to solely walking the party line for fear of losing the Party's support, that if he/she decides to act on their conscience and contrary to what the "Party" desires, he/she is not ostracized for his or her individual and personal act of conscience. When they took office, they swore allegiance to the United States of America *and not to* the Republican or Democratic Party.

Division, Divisiveness, Distrust, Dysfunction, Discord, and Dissatisfaction

In such a case as exists today, the two major parties are two too many. All that they now provide to we the people is division, divisiveness, distrust, dysfunction, discord, and dissatisfaction. Their inflammatory rhetoric has fanned the bitter flames of revenge and divided the extremes of both into separate camps, unwilling to govern together, while the majority of both parties as well as "the silent majority" of America stand mute and allow a discordant minority to rule. Better that We the People should shun our own apathy, our complacency, our silence, and move away from party loyalty and allegiance and the false belief that these *all too proud and self-indulgent* political machines know what is right. They have demonstrated otherwise, that pride, ego, individual prejudices, and party loyalty, *and not the good of we the people*, are what rules in our present Congress.

We must think and act independently, shunning *their* political rhetoric and propaganda. We must vote but vote not *blindly* for a party or personality but on our own cold, calculated, unimpassioned, thought-out principles, and remember that tolerance, compromise, and common sense, more often than not, can and will achieve the common goal of peacefully and successfully governing our nation.

Twenty-four years after President Lincoln reminded us of President Washington's warnings, an Englishman would expound on this fear of an abuse of power within government.

"Power Tends to Corrupt and Absolute Power Corrupts Absolutely"

Lord Acton, the author of the quote stated above was not a Founding Father of our Nation. He was not even an American. He was English. Yet his above statement reiterated the threat that Washington warned of ninety-one years earlier. *That* the result of the continued animosity between political parties, would be that of seeking security in the absolute power of one man.

"I cannot accept your cannon that we are not to judge Pope *[religious leaders]* and King *[political leaders]* unlike other men, with a favorable presumption that they did no wrong. If there is any presumption it is the other way against the_holders of power, increasing as the power increases. Historic responsibility [That is, the later judgment of historians] has to make up for the want of legal responsibility [That is, legal consequences during a ruler's lifetime]. Power tends to corrupt and absolute power corrupts absolutely.

"There Is No Worse Heresy than That the Office Sanctifies the Holder of It"

Great men are almost always bad men, even when they exercise influence and not authority; still more when you superadd the tendency or the certainty of corruption by authority. There's no worse heresy than that the *[political]* office sanctifies the holder of it. That is the point at which…the end learns to justify the means. You would hang a man of no position…but if what one hears is true, then Elizabeth asked the gaoler to murder Mary, and William III ordered his Scots minister to extirpate a clan.

Here are the greater names coupled with the greater crimes. You would spare these criminals, for some mysterious reason. I would hang them higher than *Haman*, for reasons of quite obvious justice; still more, still higher, for the sake of historical science...

[*Haman* was an authority figure in biblical times who used his power to influence his king to order the extermination of a whole people for a personal offense one of them did to Haman. His misuse of power was discovered by the king, and Haman was executed on the very gallows he had ordered built to hang the individual who had offended him.]

"If We Debase…Integrity…For the Sake of a Man's Influence…of His Party…Then History Serves Where It Ought to Reign; And It Serves the Worst Better than the Purest"

The *inflexible integrity of the moral code* is, to me, the secret of authority, the dignity, the utility of history. If we may debase the currency (that is, set aside the integrity with which historians should judge the past) for the sake of genius, or success, or rank, or reputation, we may debase it for the sake of a man's *[political]* influence, of his religion, of his party, of the good cause which prospers by his credit and suffers by his disgrace. Then history ceases to be a science, an arbiter of controversy, a guide of the wanderer, the upholder of…[high moral standards. Then history] serves where it ought to reign; and it serves the worst better than the purest.

(John Emerich Edward Dalberg-Acton (1834–1902),
Excerpt from "Lord Acton's Letter to
Archbishop Mandell Creighton,"
April 5, 1887,
History.hanover.edu

President George Washington as he began his second term in office established a level of conduct for all of our elected representatives when he stated,

**"If It Shall Be Found during
My Administration,
I Have In Any Instance Violated,**

**Willingly or Knowingly the
Injunction Thereof…**

**I May, Besides Incurring
Constitutional Punishments,
Be Subject to the Upbraidings of All"**

(George Washington (1732–1799), Second
Inaugural Address, March 4, 1793)

George Washington's Farewell Address
September 19, 1796

Friends and Citizens:

The period for a new election of a citizen to administer the executive government of the United States being not far distant, and the time actually has arrived when your thoughts must be employed in designating the person who is to be clothed with that important trust it appears to me proper, especially as it may conduce to a more distinct expression of the public voice, that I should now appraise you of the resolution I have formed, to decline from being considered among the number of those of whom a choice is to be made.

I beg you, at the same time, to do me justice to be assured that this resolution has not been taken without a strict regard to all the considerations appertaining to the relation which binds a dutiful citizen to his country; and that in withdrawing the tender of service, which silence in my situation might imply, I am influenced by no diminution of zeal for your future interest, no deficiency of grateful respect for your past kindness, but am supported by a full conviction that the step is compatible with both.

The acceptance of, and continuance hitherto in, the office to which your suffrages have twice called me have been a uniform sacrifice of inclination to the opinion of duty and to a deference for what appeared to be your desire. I constantly hoped that it would have been much earlier in my power, consistently with motives which I was not at liberty to disregard, to return to that retirement from which I had reluctantly drawn. The strength of my inclination to do this, previous to the last election, had even led to the preparation of an address to declare it to you; but mature reflection on the then perplexed and critical posture of our affairs with foreign nations, and the unanimous advise of persons entitled to my confidence, impelled me to abandoned the idea.

I rejoice that the state of your concerns, external as well as internal, no longer renders the pursuit of inclination incompatible with the sentiment of duty or propriety, and am persuaded, whatever par-

tiality may be retained for my services, that, in the present circumstances of our country, you will not disapprove my determination to
retire.

The impressions with which I first undertook the arduous
trust, were explained on the proper occasion. In the discharge of this
trust, I will only say, that I have with good intentions, contributed
towards the Organization and administration of the government, the
best exertions of which a very fallible judgment was capable. Not
unconscious, in the outset, of the inferiority of my qualifications,
experience in my own eyes, perhaps still more in the eyes of others,
has strengthened the motives of diffidence of myself; and every day
the increasing weight of years admonishes me more and more, that
the shade of retirement is as necessary to me as it will be welcome.
Satisfied that if any circumstances have given peculiar value to my
services, they were temporary, I have the consolation to believe, that
while choice and prudence invite me to quit the political scene, patriotism does not forbid it.

In looking forward to the moment, which is intended to termi-
nate the career of my public life, my feelings do not permit me to sus-
pend the deep acknowledgment of that debt of gratitude which I owe
to my beloved country; for the many honors it has conferred upon me;
still more for steadfast confidence with which it has supported me;
and for the opportunities I have thence enjoyed of manifesting my
inviolable attachment, by services faithful and persevering, though in
usefulness unequal to my zeal. If benefits have resulted to our country
from these services, let it always be remembered to your praise, and
as an instructive example in our annals, that, under circumstances
in which the Passions agitated in every direction were liable to mislead, amidst appearances Sometimes dubious, vicissitudes of fortune
often discouraging, in situations in which not infrequently want of
Success has countenanced the spirit of criticism, the constancy of
your support was the essential prop of the efforts, and a guarantee of
the plans by which they were affected. Profoundly penetrated with
this idea, I shall carry it with me to my grave, as a strong incitement
to unceasing vows that Heaven may continue to you the choicest
tokens of its beneficence—that your Union and brotherly affection

may be perpetual—that the free constitution, which is the work of your hands, may be sacredly maintained—that its Administration in every department may be stamped with wisdom and virtue—that, in fine, the happiness of the people of these States, under the auspices of liberty, may be made complete, by so careful a preservation and so prudent use of this blessing as will acquire to them the glory of recommending it to the applause, the affection -and adoption of every nation which is yet a stranger to it.

[His Apprehension of Danger]

Here, perhaps, I ought to stop. But a solicitude for your welfare, which cannot end but with my life, and the apprehension of danger, natural to that solicitude, urge me on an occasion like the present to offer to your solemn contemplation, and to recommend to your frequent review, some sentiments; which are the result of much reflection, of no inconsiderable observation, and which appear to me all important to the permanency of your felicity as a People. These will be offered to you with more freedom, as you can see them the disinterested warnings of a parting friend, who can possibly have no personal motive as his counsel. Nor can I forget, as an encouragement to it, your indulgent reception of my sentiments on a former and not dissimilar occasion. Interwoven as is the love of liberty with every ligament of your hearts, no recommendation of mine is necessary to fortify or confirm the attachment.

[Benefits of a National Union of the People]

The Unity of Government which constitutes you as *one people* is also now dear to you. It is justly so; for it is a main Pillar in the Edifice of your real independence, the support of your tranquility at home, your peace abroad; of your safety; of your prosperity; of that very Liberty which you so highly prize.

But as it is easy to foresee, that from different causes and from different quarters, much pains will be taken, may artifices employed, to weaken in your minds the conviction of this truth; as this is the point in your political fortress against which the batteries of internal and external enemies will most constantly and actively (though often covertly and insidiously) directed, it is of infinite moment, that you should properly estimate the immense value of your national Union, to your collective and individual happiness; that you cherish a cordial, habitual and immovable attachment to it; accustoming yourselves to think and speak of it as a Palladium of your political safety and prosperity; watching for its preservation with jealous anxiety; discountenancing whatever may suggest even a suspicion that it can in any event be abandoned; and indignantly frowning upon the first dawning of every attempt to alienate any portion of our Country from the rest, or to enfeeble the sacred ties which now link together the various parts.

For this you have every inducement of sympathy and interest. Citizens by birth or choice, of a common country, that country has a right to concentrate your affections.

The name of AMERICAN, which belongs to you, in your national capacity, must always exalt the just pride of Patriotism, more than any appellation derived from local discriminations. With slight shades of difference, you have the same Religion, Manners, Habits, and political Principles. You have in a common cause fought and triumphed together—the independence and Liberty you possess are the work of joint councils, and joint efforts—of common dangers, sufferings, and successes.

But these considerations, however powerfully they address themselves to your sensibility are greatly outweighed by those which apply more immediately to your Interest. Here every portion of our country finds the most commanding motives for carefully guarding and preserving the Union as a whole.

[Benefits of a Union with Common Government]

The *North,* in an unrestrained intercourse with the *South,* protected by the equal Laws of a common government, finds in the productions of the latter, great additional resources of maritime and commercial enterprise and precious materials of manufacturing industry.

The *South* in the same Intercourse, benefiting by the Agency of the *North,* sees its agriculture grow and its commerce expand. Turning partly into its own channels the seamen of the *North,* it finds its particular navigation invigorated; and while it contributes, in different ways, to nourish and increase the general mass of the national navigation, it looks forward to the protection of maritime strength, to which itself is unequally adapted.

The *East,* in alike intercourse with the *West,* already finds, and in the progressive improvement of interior communications, by land and water, will more and more find a vent for the commodities which it brings from abroad, or manufacturers at home.

The *West* derives from the East supplies requisite to its growth and comfort—and what is perhaps of still greater consequence, it must of necessity owe the *secure* enjoyment of indispensable *outlets* for its own productions to the weight, influence, and the future maritime strength of the Atlantic side of the Union, directed by an indissoluble community of interest as *one nation.* Any other tenure by which the *West* can hold this essential advantage, whether derived from its own separate strength, or from an apostate and unnatural connection with any foreign Power, must be intrinsically precarious.

While then every part of our country thus feels an immediate and particular interest in union, all the parts combined cannot fail to find in the united mass of means and efforts greater strength, greater resource, proportionately greater security from external danger, a less frequent interruption of their Peace by foreign Nations; and, what is of inestimable value! They must derive from Union an exemption from those broils and wars between themselves, which so frequently afflict neighboring countries, not tied together by the same government; which their own rivalships alone would be sufficient to produce, but which opposite foreign alliances, attachments, and intrigues would stimulate and imbitter. Hence likewise they will avoid the necessity of those overgrown military establishments, which under any form of Government are inauspicious to liberty, and which are to be regarded as particularly hostile to Republican

Liberty. In this sense it is, that your Union ought to be considered as a main prop of your liberty; and that the love of the one ought to endear to you the preservation of the other.

These considerations speak a persuasive language to every reflecting and virtuous mind, and exhibit the continuance of the UNION as a primary object of a Patriotic desire. Is there a doubt, whether a common government can embrace so large a sphere?

Let experience solve it. To listen to mere speculation is such a case were criminal. We are authorized to hope that a proper organization of the whole, with the auxiliary agency of governments for the respective Subdivisions, will afford a happy issue to the experiment. 'Tis well worth a fair and full experiment. With such powerful and obvious motives to Union, affecting all parts of our country, while experience shall not have demonstrated its impracticability, there will always be reason to distrust the patriotism of those, who in any quarter may endeavor to weaken its bands.

[Be Wary of Geographical Party Discrimination]

In contemplating the causes which may disturb our Union, it occurs as matter of serious concern, that any ground should have been furnished for characterizing of parties by *Geographical* discrimination—*Northern* and *Southern*—*Atlantic* and *Western*; whence designing men may endeavor to excite a belief that there is a real difference of local interests and views. One of the expedients of party to acquire influence, within particular districts, is to misrepresent the opinions and aim of other Districts. You cannot shield yourselves too much against the jealousies and heart burnings which spring from these misrepresentations. They tend to render alien to each other those who ought to be bound together by fraternal affection.

The inhabitants of our Western country have lately had a useful lesson on this head. They have seen, in the negotiation by the Executive, and in the unanimous ratification by the Senate, of the Treaty with Spain, and in the universal satisfaction at that event, throughout the United States, a decisive proof how unfounded were the suspicions propagated among them of a policy in the General

Government and in the Atlantic states unfriendly to their Interests in regard to the Mississippi. They have been witnesses to the formation of two Treaties, that with G. Britain and that with Spain, which secure to them everything they could desire, in respect to our Foreign relations, towards confirming their prosperity. Will it not be their wisdom to rely for the preservation of these advantages on the Union by which they were procured? Will they not henceforth be deaf to those advisors, if such there are, who would sever them from their Brethren and connect them with Aliens?

To the efficacy and permanency of Your Union, a government for the whole is indispensable. No alliance however strict between the parts can be an adequate substitute. They must inevitably experience the infractions and interruptions which all Alliances in all times have experienced.

[Your Present Government—Constitution]

Sensible to this momentous truth, you have improved upon your first essay, by the adoption of a Constitution of Government, better calculated than your former for an intimate Union, and for the efficacious management of your common concerns. This government, the offspring of our own choice uninfluenced and unawed, adopted upon full investigation and mature deliberation, completely free in its principles, in the distribution of its powers, uniting security with energy, and containing within itself a provision for its own amendment, has a just claim to your confidence and your support.

[Your Civil Responsibilities]

Respect for its authority, compliance with its Laws, acquiescence in is measures, are duties enjoined in the fundamental maxims of true Liberty. The basis of our political systems is the right of the people to make and alter their Constitutions of Government.

But the Constitution which at any time exists, 'till changed by an explicit and authentic act of the whole People, is sacredly obligatory to all. The very idea of the power and the right of the People to establish Government presupposes the duty of every Individual to obey the established government.

[Beware of Political Parties]

All obstructions to the execution of the laws, all combinations and associations, under whatever plausible character, with the real design to direct, control, counteract, or awe the regular deliberation and action of the Constituted authorities are destructive of this fundamental principle and of fatal tendency. They serve to organize faction, to give it an artificial and extraordinary force—to put in the place of the delegated will of the Nation, the will of party; often a small but artful and enterprising minority of the Community; and, according to the alternate triumphs of different parties, to make the public administration the Mirror of the ill concerted and incongruous projects of faction, rather than the Organ of consistent and wholesome plans digested by common councils and modified by mutual interests.

However combinations or Associations of the above description may now and then answer popular ends, they are likely, in the course of time and things, to become potent engines, by which cunning, ambitious and unprincipled men will be enabled to subvert the Power of the People, and to usurp for themselves the reins of Government; destroying afterwards the very engines which have lifted them to unjust dominion.

[Beware of Attacks on Our Constitution]

Toward the preservation of your Government and the permanency of your present happy state, it is requisite, not only that you steadily discountenance irregular oppositions to its acknowledged authority, but also that you resist with care the spirit of innovation upon its principles however specious the pretexts. One method of assault may be to effect, in the forms of the Constitution, alterations which will impair the energy of the system, and thus undermine what cannot be directly overthrown. In all the changes to which you may be invited, remember that time and habit are at least as necessary to fix the true character of Governments, as of other human institutions—that experience is the surest standard, by which to test the real tendency of the existing Constitution of a country—that facility in changes upon the credit of mere hypothesis and opinion exposes to perpetual change, from the endless variety of hypotheses and opinion; and remember, especially, that for the efficient management of your common interests, in a country so extensive as ours, a Government of as much vigor as is consistent with the perfect security of Liberty is indispensable -Liberty itself will find in such a government, with powers properly distributed and adjusted, its surest Guardian. It is indeed little else than a name, where the Government is too feeble to withstand the enterprises of faction, to confine each member of the Society within the limits prescribed by the laws, and to maintain all in the secure and tranquil enjoyment of the rights of person and property.

[Beware the Spirit of Party]

I have already intimated to you the danger of Parties in the State, with particular reference to the founding of them on Geographical discrimination. Let me now take a more comprehensive view and warn you in the most solemn manner against the baneful effects of the Spirit of Party, generally.

This spirit, unfortunately, is inseparable from our nature, having its root in the strongest passions of the human Mind. It exists under different shapes in all Governments, more or less stifled, controled, or repressed; but in those of popular form it is seen in its greatest rankness and is truly their worst enemy.

[Beware Giving Absolute Power to an Individual]

The alternate domination of one faction over another, sharpened by the spirit of revenge natural to party dissension, which in different ages and countries has perpetrated the most horrid enormities, is itself a frightful despotism. But this leads at length to a more formal and permanent despotism. The disorders and miseries, which result, gradually incline the minds of men to seek security and repose in the absolute power of an individual: and sooner or later the chief of some prevailing faction, more able or more fortunate than his competitors, turns this disposition to the purposes of his elevation, on the Ruins of Public Liberty. Without looking forward to an extremity of this kind (which nevertheless ought not to be entirely out of sight) the common and continual mischiefs of the spirit of party are sufficient to make it the interest and duty of a wise people to discourage and restrain it.

[The Spirit of Party Foments Occasionally Riot and Insurrection]

It serves always to distract the Public Councils and enfeeble the Public Administration. It agitates the Community with ill-founded jealousies and false alarms, kindles the animosity on one part against the other, foments occasionally riot and insurrection. It opens the door to foreign influence and corruption, which find a facilitated access to the government itself through the channels of party passions. Thus the policy and the will of one country, are subjected to the policy and will of another.

[The Spirit of Party Requires Uniform Vigilance]

There is an opinion that parties in free countries are useful checks upon the Administration of Government and serve to keep alive the spirit of Liberty. This within certain limits is probably true—and in Governments of a Monarchical cast Patriotism may look with indulgence, if not favor, upon the spirit of party. But in those of the popular character, in Governments purely elective, it is a spirit not to be encouraged.

From their natural tendency, it is certain there will always be enough of that spirit for any salutary purpose. And there being constant danger of excess, the effort ought to be, by force of public opinion, to mitigate and assuage it. A fire not to be quenched; it demands

a uniform vigilance to prevent its bursting into a flame, lest instead
of warming it should consume.

*[Beware of One Branch of Government
Encroaching on the Powers of Another]*

It is important, likewise, that the habits of thinking in a free
country should inspire caution, in those entrusted with its administration, to confine themselves within their respective Constitutional
spheres, avoiding in the exercise of the Powers of one department to
encroach upon another. The spirit of encroachment tends to consolidate the powers of all the departments in one, and thus create whatever the form of Government, a real despotism. A just estimate of
that love of power, and proneness to abuse it, which predominates in
the human heart is sufficient to satisfy us of the truth of this position.
The necessity of reciprocal checks in the exercise of political power;
by dividing and distributing it into different depositories, and consti-
tuting each the Guardian of the Public Weal against invasions by the
others, has been evinced by experiments ancient and modern; some
of them in our own country and under our own eyes. To preserve
them must be as necessary as to institute them.

*[Only the People Have the Power
to Amend Our Constitution]*

If in the opinion of the People, the distribution or modifica-
tion of the Constitutional Powers be in any particular wrong, let it
be corrected by an amendment in the way which the Constitution
designates. But let there by no change by usurpation; for though
this, in one instance, may be the instrument for good, it is the cus-
tomary weapon by which free governments are destroyed. The prec-
edent must always greatly overbalance in permanent evil any partial
or transient benefit which the use can at any time yield.

[The Importance of Religion and Morality to Government]

Of all the dispositions and habits which lead to political prosperity, religion and morality are indispensable supports. In vain would that man claim the tribute of Patriotism, who should labor to subvert these great Pillars of human happiness, these firmest props of the duties of Men and citizens. The mere politician equally with the pious man ought to respect and to cherish them. A volume could not trace all their connections with private and public felicity. Let it simply be asked where is the security for property, for reputation, for life, if the sense of religious obligation *desert* the oaths, which are the instruments of investigation in Courts of Justice? And let us with caution indulge the supposition, that morality can be maintained without religion. Whatever may be conceded to the influence of refined education on minds of peculiar structure—reason and experience both forbid us to expect that National morality can prevail in exclusion of religious principle

'Tis substantially true, that virtue and morality is a necessary spring of popular government. The rule indeed extends with more or less force to every species of free Government. Who that is a sincere friend to it can look with indifference upon attempts to shake the foundation of the fabric.

[The Education of Our Nation]

Promote then as an object of primary importance, Institutions for the general diffusion of knowledge. In proportion as the structure of government gives force to public opinion, it is essential that public opinion should be enlightened.

[Our National Credit and Debt]

As a very important source of strength and security cherish public credit. One method of preserving it is to use it as sparingly as possible; avoiding occasions of expense by cultivating peace, but remembering also that timely disbursements to prepare for danger frequently prevent much greater disbursements to repel it—avoiding likewise the accumulation of debt, not only by shunning occasions of expense, but by vigorous exertions in time of Peace to discharge the Debts which unavoidable wars may have occasioned, not ungenerously throwing upon posterity the burthen which we ourselves ought to bear. The execution of these maxims belongs to your Representatives, but it is necessary that Public Opinion should cooperate.

[Expect Taxes]

To facilitate to them the performance of their duty, its is essential that you should practically bear in mind, that towards the payment of debts there must be revenue—that to have revenue there must be taxes—that no taxes can be devised which are not more or less inconvenient and unpleasant—that the intrinsic embarrassment inseparable from the selection of proper objects (which is always a choice of difficulties) ought to be a decisive motive for a candid construction of the conduct of the Government in making it, and for a spirit of acquiescence in the measures for obtaining Revenue which the public exigencies may at any time dictate.

[Foreign Relations]

Observe good faith and justice towards all Nations, cultivate peace and harmony with all—Religion and morality enjoin this conduct; and can it be that good policy does not equally enjoin it? It will be worthy of a free, enlightened and, at no distant period, a great Nation, to give mankind the magnanimous and too novel example of a People always guided by an exalted justice and benevolence. Who can doubt that in the course of time and things the fruits of such a plan would richly repay any temporary advantages which might be lost by a steady adherence to it? Can it be, that Providence has not connected the permanent felicity of a Nation with its virtue? The experiment, at least, is recommended by every sentiment which ennobles human Nature. Alas! Is it rendered impossible by its vices?

In the execution of such a plan, nothing is more essential than that permanent, inveterate antipathies against particular Nations and passionate attachments for others should be excluded; and that in place of them just and amicable feelings towards all should be cultivated. The Nation, which indulges towards another a habitual hatred, or a habitual fondness, is in some degree a slave. It is a slave to its animosity or to its affection, either of which is sufficient to led it astray from its duty and its interest.

Antipathy in one Nation against another disposes each more readily to offer insult and injury, to lay hold of slight causes of umbrage, and to be haughty and intractable, when accidental or tri-fling occasions of dispute occur. Hence frequent collisions, obstinate envenomed and bloody contests. The Nation, prompted by ill will and resentment sometimes impels to War the Government, contrary to the best calculations of policy.

The Government sometimes participates in the national pro-pensity, and adopts through passion what reason would reject; at other times it makes the animosity of the nation subservient to proj-ects of hostility instigated by pride, ambition and other sinister and pernicious motives. The peace often, sometimes perhaps the Liberty, of Nations has been the victim.

So likewise, a passionate attachment of one Nation for another produces a variety of evils. Sympathy for the favorite nation, facili-tating the illusion of an imaginary common interest, in cases where no real common interest exists, and infusing into one the enmities of the other, betrays the former into a participation in the quarrels and Wars of the latter, without adequate inducement or justifica-tion: It leads also to concessions—to the favorite Nation of privileges denied to others, which is apt doubly to injure the Nation making the concessions—by unnecessarily parting with what ought to have been retained, and by exciting jealousy, ill will, and a disposition to retaliate, in the parties from whom equal privileges are withheld: And it gives to ambitious, corrupted, or deluded citizens (who devote themselves to the favorite Nation) facility to betray, or sacrifice the interests of their own country, without odium sometimes even with popularity; gilding with the appearances of a virtuous sense of obli-gation a commendable deference for public opinion, or a laudable zeal for public good, the base or foolish compliances of ambition, corruption or infatuation.

As avenues to foreign influence in innumerable ways, such attachments are particularly alarming to the truly enlightened and independent Patriot. How many opportunities do they afford to tamper with domestic factions, to practice the arts of seduction, to mislead public opinion, to influence or awe the public Councils! Such an attachment of a small or weak, towards a great and powerful Nation, dooms the former to be the satellite of the latter.

Against the insidious s of foreign influence (I conjure you to believe me fellow citizens) the jealousy of a free people ought to be *constantly* awake; since history and experience prove that foreign influence is one of the most baneful foes of Republican Government. But that jealousy to be useful must be impartial; else it becomes the instrument of the very influence to be avoided, instead of a defense against it. Excessive partiality for one foreign nation and excessive dislike of another, cause those whom they actuate to see danger only on one side, and serve to veil and even second the arts of influence on the other. Real Patriots, who may resist the intrigues of the favorite, are liable to become suspected and odious while its tools and dupes usurp the applause and confidence of the people, to surrender their interests.

The great rule of conduct for us, in regard to foreign Nations is in extending our commercial relations to have with them as little *political* connection as possible. So far as we have already formed engagements let then be fulfilled with perfect good faith. Here let us stop.

[Europe]

Europe has a set of primary interests, which to us have none, or a very remote relation. Hence she must be engaged in frequent controversies, the causes of which are essentially foreign to our concerns. Hence therefore it must be unwise in his to implicate ourselves, by artificial ties, in the ordinary vicissitudes of her politics, or the ordinary combinations and collisions of her friendships, or enmities.

Our detached and distant situation invites and enables us to pursue a different course. If we remain one people under an efficient government, the period is not far off, when we may defy material injury from external annoyance; when we may take such an attitude as will cause the neutrality we may at any time resolve upon to be scrupulously respected; when belligerent nations, under the impossibility of making acquisitions upon us, will not lightly hazard the giving us provocation; when we may choose peace or War, as our interest guided by justice shall counsel.

Why forgo the advantages of so peculiar a situation? Why quit our own to stand upon foreign ground? Why, by interweaving our destiny with that of any part of Europe, entangle our peace and prosperity in the toils of European ambition, Rivalship, Interest, Humour, or Caprice?

'Tis our true policy to steer clear of permanent Alliances, with any portion of the foreign world—So far, I mean, as we are now at liberty to do it; for let me not be understood as capable of patronizing infidelity to existing engagements. (I hold the maxim no less applicable to public than to private affairs, that honesty is always the best policy). I repeat it; therefore, let those engagements be observed in their genuine sense. But in my opinion, it is unnecessary and would be unwise to extend them.

Taking care always to keep ourselves, by suitable establishments, on a respectably defensive posture, we may safely trust to temporary alliances for extraordinary emergencies.

[Foreign Commerce]

Harmony, liberal intercourse with all Nations, are recommended by policy, humanity and interest. But even our Commercial policy should hold an equal and impartial hand; neither seeking or granting exclusive favours or preferences; consulting the natural course of things; diffusing and diversifying by gentle means the streams of commerce, but forcing nothing; establishing with Powers so disposed- in order to give trade a stable course, to define the rights of our merchants, and to enable the Government to support them—

conventional rules of intercourse, the best that present circumstances and mutual opinion will permit, but temporary, and liable to be from time abandoned or varied, as experience and circumstances shall dictate; constantly keeping in view; that 'tis folly in one Nation to look for disinterested favors from another—that it must pay with a portion of its independence for whatever it may accept under that character—that by such acceptance, it may place itself in the condition of having given equivalents for nominal favours and yet of being reproached with ingratitude for not giving more. There can be no greater error than to expect, or calculate upon real favours from Nation to Nation. 'Tis an illusion which experience must cure, which a just pride ought to discard.

*[May These Now and Then Recur
to Modify the Fury of Party Spirit]*

In offering to you, my Countrymen, these counsels of an old and affectionate friend, I dare not hope they will make the strong and lasting impression, I could wish—that they will control the usual current of the passions, or prevent our Nation from running the course which has hitherto marked the Destiny of Nations; But if I may even flatter myself, that they may be productive of some partial benefit, some occasional good, that they may now and then recur to moderate *the fury of party spirit*, to warn against the *mischiefs of foreign Intrigue*, to guard against the *Impostures of pretended patriotism*—this hope will be full recompense for the solicitude for your welfare, by which they have been dictated.

How far in the discharge of my Official duties, I have been guided by the principles which have been delineated, the public Records and other evidences of my conduct must witness to You and to the world. To myself, the assurance of my own conscience is, that I have at least believed myself to be guided by them.

[The Current European Conflict]

In relation to the still subsisting War in Europe, my proclamation of the 22d of April 1793 is the index to my plan. Sanctioned by your approving voice and by that of your Representatives in both Houses of Congress, the spirit of that measure has continually governed me; uninfluenced by any attempts to deter or divert me from it.

After deliberate examination with the aid of the best lights I could obtain I was well satisfied that our country, under all the circumstances of the case, had a right to take, and was bound in duty and interest, to take a Neutral position. Having taken it, I determined, as far as should depend on me, to maintain it, with moderation, perseverance and firmness.

The considerations which respect the right to hold this conduct, it is not necessary on this occasion to detail. I will only observe, that according to my understanding of the matter, that right, so far from being denied by any of the Belligerent Powers had been virtually admitted by all.

The duty of holding a Neutral conduct may be inferred, without anything more, from the obligation which justice and humanity impose on every Nation, in cases in which it is free to act, to maintain inviolate the relations of Peace and amity towards other Nations. The inducements of interest for observing that conduct will best be referred to your own reflections and experience. With me, a predominant motive has been to endeavor to gain time to our country to settle and mature its yet recent institutions, and to progress without interruption, to that degree of strength and consistency, which is necessary to give it, humanely speaking, the command of its own fortunes.

[Closing]

Though in reviewing the incidents of my Administration, I am unconscious of intentional error—I am nevertheless too sensible of my defects not to think it probable that I may have committed many errors. Whatever they may be I fervently beseech the Almighty to avert or mitigate the evils to which they may tend. I shall also carry

with me the hope that my Country will never cease to view them
with indulgence; and that after forty-five years of my life dedicated
to its Service, with an upright zeal, the faults of incompetent abilities
will be consigned to oblivion, as myself must soon be to the man-
sions of rest. Relying on its kindness in this as in other things, and
actuated by that fervent love towards it, which is so natural to a man
who views in it the native soil of himself and his progenitors for sev-
eral Generations; I anticipate with pleasing expectation that retreat,
in which I promise myself to realize, without alloy, the sweet enjoyment of partaking, in the midst of my fellow Citizens, the benign
influence of good Laws under a free Government—the ever favorite
object of my heart, and the happy reward, as I trust, of our mutual
cares, labors and dangers.

Assembled for You
THE PEOPLE
For "your" reading and knowledge
And
For the sake of our nation, our constitution,
our Bill of Rights, and our posterity

Your respectful servant,
B. Cylent Knowmohr

Quote Attributions

Abraham Lincoln's quote from "Lincoln's Lost Speech" (1838)
In public domain within the United States
Source: https://archive.org/details/lifeworsk02lincuoft /page 275 of 302

William Pitt the Elder quote from 1770
In public domain within the United States
Source: https://wikiquote.org/wiki_Pitt_1st_Earl_of_Chatham

George Washington quote from His "Farewell Address" (9/15/1796)
In public domain within the United States
"Farewell Address, 19 September 1796," *Founders Online*, National Archives, https://founders.archives.gov/documents/Washinghton/05-20-0-0440-0002.
Original source: The Papers of George Washington, Presidential Series, vol. 20 1 April–21 September 1796, ed. David R. Hoth and William M. Ferraro. Charlottesville: University of Virginia Press, 2019. pp. 703–722

John Adams letter to Jonathan Jackson (October 2, 1780)
In public domain within the United States
Cite as "From John Adams to Jonathan Jackson, 2 October 1780," *Founders Online*, National Archives, https://founders.archives.gov/documents/Adams/o6-10-02-0113
Original source: The Adams Papers, Papers of John Adams, vol. 10 July 1780–December 1780 ed. Gregg L. Lint and Richard Alan Ryerson. Cambridge, MA: Harvard University Press, 1996, pp. 192–193.

James Madison quote from Federalist Papers #10 (11/22/1787)
In public domain within the United States
The Library of Congress; Alexander Hamilton, James Madison, John Jay, an American Imprint Collection by Samuel Harrison Smith and Peter Force. The Federalist: a collection of essays, written

in favor of the new Constitution, as agreed upon by the Federal
Convention; in two volumes. New York: Printed and sold by
John Tiebout, 1799 Pdlf. https//www.loc.gov/item(09021561/.

James Madison quote from Federalist Papers #10 (11/22/1787)
In public domain within the United States
The Library of Congress; Alexander Hamilton, James Madison, John
    Jay, an American Imprint Collection by Samuel Harrison Smith
    and Peter Force. The Federalist: a collection of essays, written
    in favor of the new Constitution, as agreed upon by the Federal
    Convention; in two volumes. New York: Printed and sold by
    John Tiebout, 1799 Pdlf. https//www.loc.gov/item(09021561/.

Thomas Jefferson quote from letter to Francis Hopkins (03/13/1789)
In public domain within the United States
From Thomas Jefferson to Francis Hopkinson, 13 March 1789,
    Founders Online, National Archives https://founders.archives.
    gov/documents/Jefferson/-1-14-02-0402
Original Source: *The Papers of Thomas Jefferson, vol.14, 8 October
    1788–26 March 1789, ed. Juian P. Byd. Princeton University
    Press, 1958 pp. 649–651.*

Alexander Hamilton quote from Federalist Papers #1 (10/27/1787)
In public domain within the United States
The Library of Congress; Alexander Hamilton, James Madison, John
    Jay, an American Imprint Collection by Samuel Harrison Smith
    and Peter Force. The Federalist: a collection of essays, written
    in favor of the new Constitution, as agreed upon by the Federal
    Convention; in two volumes. New York: Printed and sold by
    John Tiebout, 1799 Pdlf. https//www.loc.gov/item(09021561/.

Alexander Hamilton quote from Federalist Papers #1 (10/27/1787)
In public domain within the United States
The Library of Congress; Alexander Hamilton, James Madison, John
    Jay, an American Imprint Collection by Samuel Harrison Smith
    and Peter Force. The Federalist: a collection of essays, written

in favor of the new Constitution, as agreed upon by the Federal Convention; in two volumes. New York: Printed and sold by John Tiebout, 1799 Pdlf. https//www.loc.gov/item(09021561/.

James Madison quote from Federalist Papers #10 (11/22/1787)
In public domain within the United States
The Library of Congress; Alexander Hamilton, James Madison, John Jay, an American Imprint Collection by Samuel Harrison Smith and Peter Force. The Federalist: a collection of essays, written in favor of the new Constitution, as agreed upon by the Federal Convention; in two volumes. New York: Printed and sold by John Tiebout, 1799 Pdlf. https//www.loc.gov/item(09021561/.

John Jay quote from Federalist Papers #5 (11/10/1787)
In public domain within the United States
The Library of Congress; Alexander Hamilton, James Madison, John Jay, an American Imprint Collection by Samuel Harrison Smith and Peter Force. The Federalist: a collection of essays, written in favor of the new Constitution, as agreed upon by the Federal Convention; in two volumes. New York: Printed and sold by John Tiebout, 1799 Pdlf. https//www.loc.gov/item(09021561/.

Thomas Jefferson quote from his 1st Inaugural Address (3/4/1801)
In public domain within the United States
Cite as "Editorial Note: First Inaugural Address," *Founders Online*, National Archives, https://founders.archives.goov/documents/Jefferson/01-33-02-0116-0001.
Original source: The Papers of Thomas Jefferson, vol. 33, 17 February–30 April 1801, ed. Barbara B. Oberg, Princeton: Princeton University Press, 2006, pp. 134–138.

Alexander Hamilton quote from Federalist Paper #85 (3/16/1788)
In public domain within the United States
The Library of Congress; Alexander Hamilton, James Madison, John Jay, an American Imprint Collection by Samuel Harrison Smith and Peter Force. The Federalist: a collection of essays, written

in favor of the new Constitution, as agreed upon by the Federal Convention; in two volumes. New York: Printed and sold by John Tiebout, 1799 Pdlf. https//www.loc.gov/item(09021561/.

George Washington quote from His "Farewell Address" (9/15/1796)
In public domain within the United States
"Farewell Address, 19 September 1796," *Founders Online*, National Archives, https://founders.archives.gov/documents/ Washinghton/05-20-0-0440-0002.
Original source: The Papers of George Washington, Presidential Series, vol. 20 1 April–21 September 1796, ed. David R. Hoth and William M. Ferraro. Charlottesville: University of Virginia Press, 2019. pp. 703–722.

George Washington quote from His "Farewell Address" (9/15/1796)
In public domain within the United States
Cite as "Farewell Address, 19 September 1796," *Founders Online*, National Archives, https://founders.achives.gov/docyments/ Washington/05-20-02-0440-0002.
Original source: *The Papers of George Washington*, Presidential Series, vol. 20 1 April–21 September 1796, ed. David R. Hoth and William M. Ferraro. Charlottesville: University of Virginia Press, 2019, pp. 703–722.

George Washington quote from His "Farewell Address" (9/15/1796)
In public domain within the United States
Cite as "Farewell Address, 19 September 1796," *Founders Online*, National Archives, https://founders.achives.gov/docyments/ Washington/05-20-02-0440-0002.
Original source: *The Papers of George Washington*, Presidential Series, vol. 20 1 April–21 September 1796, ed. David R. Hoth and William M. Ferraro. Charlottesville: University of Virginia Press, 2019, pp. 703–722.]

George Washington quote from His "Farewell Address" (9/15/1796)
In public domain within the United States

Cite as "Farewell Address, 19 September 1796," *Founders Online*, National Archives, https://founders.achives.gov/docyments/ Washington/05-20-02-0440-0002.
Original source: *The Papers of George Washington*, Presidential Series, vol. 20 1 April–21 September 1796, ed. David R. Hoth and William M. Ferraro. Charlottesville: University of Virginia Press, 2019, pp. 703–722.

Alexander Hamilton quote from the Farmer Refuted (2/23/1775)
In public domain within the United States
Cite as "The Farmer Refuted &c., 23 February 1775," Founders Online, National Archives. https://founders.archives.gov/ documents/Hamilton/01-01-02-0057.
Original source: The Papers of Alexander Hamilton, vol. 1, 1768-1778, ed. Harold C. Syrett. New York: Columbia University Press, 1961, pp. 81–165.

George Washington quote from His "Farewell Address" (9/15/1796)
In public domain within the United States
Cite as "Farewell Address, 19 September 1796," *Founders Online*, National Archives, https://founders.achives.gov/docyments/ Washington/05-20-02-0440-0002.
Original source: *The Papers of George Washington*, Presidential Series, vol. 20 1 April–21 September 1796, ed. David R. Hoth and William M. Ferraro. Charlottesville: University of Virginia Press, 2019, pp. 703–722.]

Alexander Hamilton quote from "Objections and Answers Respecting the Administration" (08/18/1792)
In public domain within the United States. Copyright held by Library of Congressional.
Cite as "Enclosure:[Objections and Answers Respecting the Administration]," Founders Online, National Archives, https:// founders.archives.gov/documents   *Hamilton*01-12-02-0184-0002.

Original Source: The papers of Alexander Hamilton, vol.12, July 1792–October 1792, ed. Harold C. Syrett. New York: Columbia University Press, 1967.

Alexander Hamilton quote from "Objections and Answers Respecting the Administration" (08/18/1792)
In public domain within the United States. Copyright held by Library of Congressional.
Cite as "Enclosure: [Objections and Answers Respecting the Administration]," Founders Online, National Archives, https://founders.archives.gov/documents *Hamilton*01-12-02-0184-0002.
Original Source: The papers of Alexander Hamilton, vol. 12, July 1792–October 1792, ed. Harold C. Syrett. New York: Columbia University Press, 1967, pp. 29–258.

James Madison quote from Federalist Papers #10 (11/22/1787)
In public domain within the United States
The Library of Congress; Alexander Hamilton, James Madison, John Jay, an American Imprint Collection by Samuel Harrison Smith and Peter Force. The Federalist: a collection of essays, written in favor of the new Constitution, as agreed upon by the Federal Convention; in two volumes. New York: Printed and sold by John Tiebout, 1799 Pdlf. https//www.loc.gov/item(09021561/.

Alexander Hamilton quote from Federalist Papers #1 (10/27/1787)
In public domain within the United States
The Library of Congress; Alexander Hamilton, James Madison, John Jay, an American Imprint Collection by Samuel Harrison Smith and Peter Force. The Federalist: a collection of essays, written in favor of the new Constitution, as agreed upon by the Federal Convention; in two volumes. New York: Printed and sold by John Tiebout, 1799 Pdlf. https//www.loc.gov/item(09021561/.

George Washington quote from His "Farewell Address" (8/15/1796)
In public domain within the United States

Cite as "Farewell Address, 19 September 1796," *Founders Online*, National Archives, https://founders.achives.gov/docyments/Washington/05-20-02-0440-0002.

Original source: *The Papers of George Washington*, Presidential Series, vol. 20 1 April–21 September 1796, ed. David R. Hoth and William M. Ferraro. Charlottesville: University of Virginia Press, 2019, pp. 703–722.

Alexander Hamilton quote from "Objections and Answers Respecting the Administration" (08/18/1792)

In public domain within the United States. Copyright held by Library of Congressional.

Cite as "Enclosure:[Objections and Answers Respecting the Administration]," Founders Online, National Archives, https://founders.archives.gov/documents *Hamilton*01-12-02-0184-0002.

Original Source: The papers of Alexander Hamilton, vol.12, July 1792-October 1792, ed.

Alexander Hamilton quote from "Objections and Answers Respecting the Administration" (08/18/1792)

In public domain within the United States. Copyright held by Library of Congressional.

Cite as "Enclosure:[Objections and Answers Respecting the Administration]," Founders Online, National Archives, https://founders.archives.gov/documents *Hamilton*01-12-02-0184-0002.

Original Source: The papers of Alexander Hamilton, vol.12, July 1792–October 1792, ed. Harold C. Syrett. New York: Columbia University Press, 1967, pp. 29–258.

Alexander Hamilton quote from "Objections and Answers Respecting the Administration" (08/18/1792)

In public domain within the United States. Copyright held by Library of Congressional.

Cite as "Enclosure:[Objections and Answers Respecting the Administration]," Founders Online, National Archives, https://founders.archives.gov/documents *Hamilton*01-12-02-0184-0002.

Original Source: The papers of Alexander Hamilton, vol.12, July 1792–October 1792, ed. Harold C. Syrett. New York: Columbia University Press, 1967, pp. 29–258.

Alexander Hamilton quote from Federalist Paper #9 (11/21/1787)
In public domain within the United States
The Library of Congress; Alexander Hamilton, James Madison, John Jay, an American Imprint Collection by Samuel Harrison Smith and Peter Force. The Federalist: a collection of essays written in favor of the new Constitution, as agreed upon by the Federal Convention; in two volumes. New York: Printed and sold by John Tiebout, 1799 Pdlf. https//www.loc.gov/item(09021561/.

George Washington quote from His "Farewell Address" (9/15/1796)
In public domain within the United States
Cite as "Farewell Address, 19 September 1796," *Founders Online*, National Archives, https://founders.achives.gov/docyments/ Washington/05-20-02-0440-0002.

Original source: *The Papers of George Washington*, Presidential Series, vol. 20 1 April–21 September 1796, ed. David R. Hoth and William M. Ferraro. Charlottesville: University of Virginia Press, 2019, pp. 703–722.]

George Washington quote from His "Farewell Address" (9/15/1796)
In public domain within the United States
Cite as "Farewell Address, 19 September 1796," *Founders Online*, National Archives, https://founders.achives.gov/docyments/ Washington/05-20-02-0440-0002.

Original source: *The Papers of George Washington*, Presidential Series, vol. 20 1 April–21 September 1796, ed. David R. Hoth and William M. Ferraro. Charlottesville: University of Virginia Press, 2019, pp. 703–722.

Thomas Pain quote from "Opposers to the Bank" (3/17/1787)
In the public domain within the United States
Source: The Thomas Paine National Historical Association

Benjamin Franklin quote from letter to Abbess Chalut and Anaud
    (4/17/1787)
In the public domain within the United States
Source: AZ Quotes, "TOP 25 Benjamin Franklin Quotes on Liberty"

Benjamin Franklin quote from Speech to Convention (9/17/1787)
In the public domain within the United States
Source: National Constitution Center, Historic Document, "Closing
    Speech at the Constitutional Convention" (1787).

John Jay's "Federalist Paper No. 4" (11/7/1777)
In the public domain within the United States
Source: Library of Congress webpage,
https://www.loc.gov/item/federalist-papers/full-text?ref=upstract.com.

John Jay's "Federalist Paper No. 5" (11/10/1777)
In the public domain within the United States
Source: Library of Congress webpage,
https://www.loc.gov/item/federalist-papers/full-text?ref=upstract.com.

Thomas Jefferson quote from "Notes to the State of Virginia"
    (1781–1783)
In the public domain in the United States.
Source: Library of Congress, https://www.loc.gov/item/03004904.

Benjamin Franklin quote from his "A Historical Review of the
    Constitution and Government of Pennsylvania" (1759)
In public domain within the United States

Thomas Paine quote from his pamphlet "Common Sense" (2/19/1776)
In public domain within the United States
Source: National Constitution Center, https://constitutioncenter.org.

John Adams quote from his letter to Abigail Adams (8/26/1777)
In public domain within the United States
Cite as "John Adams to Abigail Adams, 26 April 1777." Founders
    Online, National Archives, https://founders.archives.gov/
    documents/Adams/04-02-02-0169.
Original Source: The Adams paper, Adams Family Correspondence.
    Vol. 2 June 1776–March 1778, ed. L. H. Butterfieldf,
    Cambridge, MA: Harvard University Press 1963, pp. 223–224.

Abraham Lincoln's "Lyceum Address" (1/27/1838)
In public domain within the United States
    Source: https://archive.org/details/lifewlrks02linoft/page14 of 30

Lord Acton quote from his letter to Archbishop Creigton (4/5/1887)
Online Library of Liberty; in public domain within the United States

George Washington quote from his 2nd inaugural address (3/4/1793)
In public domain within the United States
Cite as "Second Inaugural Address, 4 March 1793," *Founders Online*,
    National Archives, https: founders.archives.gov/documents/
    Washington/o5-12-02-0200.
Original source: The Papers of George Washington, Presidential
    Series, vol. 12, 16 January 1793–31 May 1793, ed. Christine
    Sternberg Patrick and John C. Pinheiro. Charlottesville:
    University of Virginia Press, 2005, pp. 26–265.

George Washington's Farewell Address (9/19/1796)
In Public Domain within the United States
Source: Founders Online
Cite As: "Farewell Address," 19 September 1796, Founders Online,
    National Archives, https//founders.archives.gov/docyments/
    Washington/05-20-02-0440-0002.
Original source: *The Papers of George Washington*, Presidential Series,
    vol. 20, 1 April–21 September 1796, ed. David R. Hoth and
    William M. Ferraro. Charlottesville: University of Virginia
    Press, 2019, pp.703-722.

Image Permissions

The images displayed in this book were sourced from www.shutterstock.com under a standard license issued on January 18, 2024.

- George Washington, 1006711357
- Alexander Hamilton, 1445770067
- John Adams, 2328869265
- Thomas Jefferson, 1443371885
- Abraham Lincoln, 777082
- James Madison, 2329098301
- Thomas Paine, 1450504754
- Benjamin Franklin, 1204190602
- John Jay, 1339888730

About the Author

B. Cylent Knowmohr is American citizen seeking the anonymity used by many of the Founding Fathers during their lifetimes—men such as Benjamin Franklin using the pseudonym of Silence Dogood in 1722 and the pseudonym of Publius used by Alexander Hamilton, John Jay, and James Madison when writing the *Federalist Papers* between 1787 and 1788. It was the messages being conveyed and not the authorship they believed important.

He hopes the reader will get to know more about our Forefather's thoughts concerning the political parties leading us during these tumultuous times and to inspire the reader to reflect upon *our individual roles* in the continuance of our republican system of government, *especially* when *radical* party members are sowing discord, dysfunction, disinformation, and wild threats of succession.